Retaining Employees

Pocket Mentor Series

The Pocket Mentor Series offers immediate solutions to common challenges managers face on the job every day. Each book in the series is packed with handy tools, self-tests, and real-life examples to help you identify your strengths and weaknesses and hone critical skills. Whether you're at your desk, in a meeting, or on the road, these portable guides enable you to tackle the daily demands of your work with greater speed, savvy, and effectiveness.

Books in the series:

Retaining Employees

Expert Solutions to Everyday Challenges

Harvard Business Review Press

Boston, Massachusetts

Library of Congress Cataloging-in-Publication Data

Retaining employees : expert solutions to everyday challenges.
    p. cm. — (Pocket mentor series)
  Includes bibliographical references.
  ISBN 978-1-4221-2972-2 (pbk. : alk. paper) 1. Employee retention.
  HF5549.5.R58R486 2010
  658.3'14—dc22

                              2010000933

Contents

Retention Strategy 1: Hiring Right   21

Tips for bringing the right people on board.

Retention Strategy 2: Making Your Company an Employer of Choice   31

Ideas for making valued employees want to stay.

Retention Strategy 3: Retaining a Multigenerational Workforce   51

Strategies for keeping employees from different generations on board.

Retention Strategy 4: Cultivating the Right Culture   61

Suggestions for crafting an appealing culture.

Retention Strategy 5: Helping Employees Avoid Burnout   67

Advice for combating an all-too-common workplace scourge.

To Learn More   119

Further titles of articles and books if you want to go more deeply into the topic.

Sources for Retaining Employees   127

Mentors' Message: Why Is Employee Retention Important?

Quick: What's one of the best things you can do for your organization? It's keeping valued employees on board. No matter what's going on in the larger economy, companies are always at risk of losing their best employees to rivals. And when talented workers defect, their knowledge and expertise—so crucial to your company's success—go with them. Equally destructive, your firm must shell out hefty sums to replace departing employees and get the new hires up to speed.

Become a retention champ, and you help position your company to succeed in an ever more competitive world. In this book, you'll discover what employee retention is (and isn't), why it's so important today, and why it's more challenging than ever. You'll then learn specific strategies for retaining valued employees: hiring right, making your company an employer of choice, cultivating the right culture, helping employees avoid burnout, and strengthening your retention skills overall.

Learning how to retain your employees takes practice and effort—but the results are well worth it: a high-performing, motivated, and fulfilled team that can help bring your company to new levels of success.

James Waldroop and Timothy Butler, Mentors

James Waldroop is a principal and cofounder of CareerLeader, LLP. Until 2001, he was codirector of MBA Career Development Programs at Harvard Business School. Jim's work focuses on two areas of interface between psychology and the world of business: individual management development (executive effectiveness development) and career development assessment and counseling.

Timothy Butler is a Senior Fellow and Director of Career Development Programs at Harvard Business School. His research interests focus on career decision making in general and the relationship between personality structure and work satisfaction in particular. His most recent book is *Getting Unstuck: A Guide to Discovering Your Next Career Path* (Harvard Business Press, 2010).

Waldroop and Butler spent many years helping business people work through the career planning and development processes, including developing the Internet-based interactive career assessment program CareerLeader currently used by over four hundred MBA programs and corporations around the world. Waldroop and Butler are also the authors of four *Harvard Business Review* articles and two books: *Discovering Your Career in Business* (Perseus, 1997) and *The 12 Bad Habits That Hold Good People Back* (Doubleday, 2001).

Retaining Employees: The Basics

An Overview of Employee Retention

The subject of employee retention gets a lot of attention within organizations and in the business press. But what is it, exactly? Why is it more important than ever for today's businesses? And what enhances—and what discourages—retention? In the following pages, we explore these questions.

What is retention?

Retention refers to a company's ability to keep talented employees—people who will help their organization remain competitive in a world of rapid change. From an organization's point of view, retention doesn't mean trying to hang on to every employee forever. It means keeping good employees for the *most appropriate amount of time for their particular function or level.*

For example, with some jobs, such as entry-level computer programming, the ideal tenure may be just two years. By allowing people to move on after that time span, your firm can then hire newcomers who have the most up-to-date educational background or technical expertise and who may cost less in terms of salary than more seasoned personnel.

One thing that retention is *not* is continuing to invest in employees who, for whatever reason, aren't contributing in positive ways to the company.

The importance of retention can also vary widely from culture to culture. For instance, in some countries, employees tend to stay at one company for their entire professional lives, while in other countries, they move from firm to firm frequently, depending on available opportunities and their interests and priorities.

Even within one culture or country (or within one geographic region), attention to keeping good employees may fluctuate, depending on economic conditions and shifting workplace realities.

Why is retention crucial?

For several reasons, retaining good employees counts among the most essential ingredients for success in today's business world.

Companies depend on intellectual capital. In these times of accelerating change, it's not machines or financial assets that companies depend on to survive and thrive, but the people who acquire, build on, and use knowledge to keep the organization competitive. Today's successful businesses win with innovative new ideas and top-notch products and services—all of which stem from employees' knowledge and skills, or their *intellectual capital*. Examples of people who possess intellectual capital include:

- Computer programmers
- Network engineers
- Technical designers
- Direct-marketing analysts

Other employees whose intellectual capital makes them high-value company assets are:

- Midlevel managers (they know whom to contact to get things done)

- Top-level executives (they have years of business savvy and industry knowledge)

- Strategic-planning/business-development professionals (they know how to do competitive and other crucial analyses)

- Human resource professionals (they know about recruiting, employment law, compensation, and other critical employee-relations issues)

- In-house legal counsel (they may know about intellectual property, securities, and other areas of the law—and they know whom to consult for specialized advice if necessary)

When high-value employees leave, your company loses their hard-won knowledge and (often expensively) acquired skills. When those employees go to companies that yours competes with in the marketplace, the damage to your firm is compounded. Not only has your company lost intellectual capital, but your competitors have *gained* it—without having to invest the time and dollars in training that your firm may have invested.

More people are leaving companies. Retention is also more crucial today than ever because organizations are finding it increasingly difficult to keep their best employees. Some recent statistics reveal just how critical the issue of employee retention is. According to one study:

- As many as 33% of employees—one in three—are "high risk"; that is, they're not committed to their present employer and are not planning to stay for the next two years.

- About four in ten—39%—feel "trapped"; they aren't committed to the organization, but they're currently planning to stay for the next two years.

- Only 24%—about one in four—are "truly loyal"; they're committed to the organization and are planning to stay on for at least two years.

Clearly, an alarming number of employees would like to (or are planning to) leave their companies.

Replacing employees is costly. The cost of employee turnover involves a lot more than just lost training dollars. Whenever your firm loses a valued worker and then tries to replace him or her, it can incur these costs as well:

- Search expenses, including search firms, newspaper ads, and so on

- Direct interview expenses (for instance, airfares, hotels, meals)

- Managers' and team members' time spent interviewing

- Work put on hold until a replacement is hired and trained

- Overload on teams, including overtime, to get work done during the time it takes to select and train a replacement

- Overburdened team members' lower morale and productivity

- Sign-on bonus, moving allowance, and other perks for replacement

- Orientation and training time spent on replacement

- Initial low productivity of new employee during start-up period (often six to twelve months)

- Potential lost customers, contracts, or business

- Potential loss of other employees (their departure activates the all-too-common "domino effect," in which one employee's departure inspires other employees to leave)

In sheer dollar terms, the cost of employee turnover may shock you: All told, replacing an employee is likely to cost your firm *twice the departee's annual salary—at least!*

Employee defections erode customer satisfaction and profitability. Losing a good employee carries another kind of price tag as well: the erosion of customer satisfaction and—ultimately—customer profitability. How does this work? The longer employees stay with your firm, the more they get to know the company's customers (or their internal clients)—their likes, dislikes, special problems or needs, and the unique factors that keep them loyal. Customers get to know frontline employees, too, and appreciate hearing or seeing a familiar voice or face whenever they do business with your firm.

If those familiar employees leave, customers may not get the same quality of service they're used to. If they become dissatisfied as a result, they'll defect to other companies. Thus the cost of losing an employee can be greatly compounded by the resultant loss of customers.

The statistics behind these trends are startling: Most companies lose half their employees in three to four years—and half their customers in five. In an era when every loyal customer counts, your firm simply can't afford to lose the high-quality employees who keep those customers loyal.

> *Leaders view their best employees as they do their best customers:*
> *Once they've got them, they do everything possible to keep them.*
> —Frederick F. Reichheld

Why do employees stay with a company?

People stay with a company for many different reasons, which vary widely from culture to culture. However, in cultures in which it's assumed that people may freely change jobs, the *major* motivations for staying are:

- **Pride in the organization:** People want to work for well-managed companies headed by skilled, resourceful leaders—that is, top-level managers who have a clear vision of the firm's future, who can devise powerful strategies for success, and who can motivate others to realize that vision.

- **Compatible supervisor:** Even more important is employees' immediate relationship with their supervisor. People may stay just to work for a particular individual who is supportive of them.

- **Compensation:** People also want to work for companies that offer fair compensation. This includes not only competitive wages and benefits but also intangible compensation in the form of opportunities to learn, grow, and achieve.

- **Affiliation:** The chance to work with respected and compatible colleagues is another element that many people consider essential.

- **Meaningful work:** Finally, people want to work for companies that let them do the kinds of work that appeal to their deepest, most passionate interests.

Why do employees leave?

People typically leave an organization because conditions change. For example:

- Either the quality of top management's decisions declines, or new leaders—whom employees don't yet trust or feel comfortable with—take the helm. People may also leave because their relationship with their own supervisor becomes too stressful or problematic, and they don't see any other options in their company.

- One or more colleagues whom an employee particularly likes and respects leaves the firm, thus taking away the affiliation that means so much to that employee.

- A person's job responsibilities change so that the work no longer appeals to his or her deepest interests or provides a sense of profound meaning or stimulation.

But perhaps the more central point to keep in mind when thinking about why people leave is this: *People most often leave for the wrong reasons.* That is, they leave without really understanding why they're unhappy or what opportunities to improve things may exist within the company. Thus they jump from company to company, making the same mistake each time.

For example, an engineer is promoted to a managerial position because she's a high performer who has been at the company for a while. This person may not even like being a manager. But she hasn't yet identified her deepest work interests, so she doesn't make the connection between her new role and her unhappiness. Instead, she concludes that she just doesn't like the company anymore—and starts looking for another job. Unfortunately, when she finds another job outside the company, it'll likely be another managerial position. So, she'll work at that job for a while but then realize that she's still unhappy—and decide that the new company, too, is a bad fit for her.

> *Fifty-three percent of U.S. workers expect to voluntarily leave their jobs in the next five years.*
> —Jim Harris and Joan Brannick

Understanding the Challenges to Retaining Employees

As retention has become more important to organizations, it has also become more challenging, owing to several developments. These include demographic changes, new economic realities, cultural expectations, and upheavals in the world of work.

Demographic changes

In some countries, most notably the United States, demographic changes have made retention especially difficult. Here are just a few of the more remarkable statistics from the American scene:

- The workforce overall is maturing, with the average age of employees rising from 35 to 55.

- The economy has been growing overall more than the workforce.

- The population of Americans in the prime management age range of 35–45 is decreasing.

The ramifications of these trends? A pronounced shortage of skilled workers—and an escalating competition among companies to recruit and retain those who are available.

New economic realities

Many areas of the world are experiencing some dramatic economic shifts. For example, in some countries, the unemployment rate is falling while the economy is flourishing. During such boom times, businesses have plenty of money to fund the high salaries and perks that will lure desirable employees away from competitors.

What happens when you put the above two trends together—a tight labor market and a surplus of cash-rich, worker-hungry companies? You get a true "war for talent," in which attracting and keeping good employees becomes increasingly difficult for everyone. As a result, employee turnover rates mount.

Cultural expectations

People's expectations about work are also strongly influencing retention patterns. For example, in some countries, or geographic regions within a country, companies *and* employees expect that people will work for one firm during their entire professional lifetime. Employees, their colleagues, and employers consider one another almost as family, and give each other the same dedication, commitment, and support that one would give family members. In other places, the culture emphasizes fast-moving and continual change—including rapid "job-hopping" by workers in search of the best possible combination of work, compensation, and opportunity.

In addition, some countries' employment laws make it very difficult for companies to fire or lay off workers. In other places, however, companies can let employees go easily without a required safety net such as a severance package.

?

What Would YOU Do?

Flight of an Angel?

R ICHARD WAS AN engineering manager at Winthrop Aviation Technologies. He had recently conducted a performance appraisal for Angel, one of his best employees. He assumed she would be pleased with the appraisal. His feedback was positive, plus he had given her a raise and a promotion.

Her reaction was totally unexpected. True, she had thanked him for the pay increase and new title, but then she had said that she was thinking about doing something else—and that her work wasn't fulfilling anymore.

Richard thought to himself, "How could she be dissatisfied with her job when she's so good at it?" He wondered, "Should I offer her more money?" He hated to think about losing her; in fact, the company had lost several high performers lately, and management was becoming concerned. But he wasn't sure how best to persuade her to stay.

What would YOU do? The mentors will suggest a solution in *What You COULD Do*.

Finally, some cultures expect primarily men to hold paid work positions outside the home. For others, the composition of the workforce in terms of gender, age, ethnic, or racial makeup, and so on, changes with other major historical shifts. For example, in the

United States, the government encouraged women to obtain paid work outside the home during World War II. After that conflict, women continued to pour into the workforce in unprecedented numbers.

As you might guess, a company's retention goals might be more or less challenging depending on the cultural factors that are shaping employment trends in the industry and the region where the enterprise does business.

Upheavals in the world of work

Upheavals in the world of work are also making retention increasingly challenging. Here are just a few examples:

- **A trend toward free agency.** Free agents—self-employed workers who serve various clients on a temporary, contract basis—make up a growing percentage of some countries' workforces.

- **The dissolving of the old employer/employee contract.** With the wave of reengineering and restructuring that hit many parts of the business world back in the 1970s and 1980s, some companies downplayed the importance of the workforce. As a result, old assumptions about the employer as protector and the employee as loyal devotee evaporated. Now, workers who experienced this shift assume (correctly) that it's up to them to take charge of their own employ-ability and careers—even if that means moving from firm to firm to get the best work and compensation package. In the United States alone, for example, most people will hold as many as 8.6 different jobs between the ages of 18 and 32.

- **A growth in Internet recruiting.** The Internet has made it easier than ever for employees to learn about—and apply for—jobs at other companies.

When you put these trends together, it's clear that companies can no longer expect employees to join them early in life and stay indefinitely. Instead, firms must actively and creatively encourage good people to stay—especially in high-tech markets.

How to beat the challenges

To beat these challenges and improve retention in your firm, you can't rely on traditional strategies such as the following:

- **Counteroffering when an employee gives notice.** This tactic misses the point about what really causes people to leave. Most employees don't leave purely for a bigger paycheck. So, by presenting a counteroffer, managers make it even more painfully clear that they don't understand employees' real needs. And if the counteroffer *does* persuade the employee to stay, he or she will likely attempt to leave again eventually— because the manager hasn't addressed the root of that individual's dissatisfaction.

- **Exit interviews.** During exit interviews, companies routinely ask employees why they're leaving. But this just scratches the surface of attrition problems. During exit interviews, most employees report on what's attractive about their new job—without explaining why they were looking in the first place. (Hint: It likely had nothing to do with compensation.) Moreover, departing employees rarely give the real reasons they're leaving—for fear of retribution or of damaging relationships in a way that will later hurt their professional standing.

To keep your best workers, you need to use much more effective strategies. In the sections that follow, we'll examine five especially potent ones:

- Hiring right

- Making your company an employer of choice

- Cultivating the right culture

- Helping employees avoid burnout

- Strengthening your retention skills

?What You COULD Do.

Remember Richard's concern about how best to keep Angel on board?

Here's what the mentors suggest:

Richard should talk with Angel to better understand why she no longer finds her work fulfilling. His goal is to ask questions and uncover the root cause of her dissatisfaction. By digging deeper, Richard can learn what Angel would consider improvements in her current job duties. For example, perhaps Angel would like to lead others, work more with language, or take on more assignments that require creativity. He can then explore opportunities to "sculpt" Angel's job to better match her interests or perhaps to identify more satisfying opportunities for her within the company—to retain this valuable employee.

Retention Strategy 1: Hiring Right

The hiring process provides a valuable opportunity for you to lay the foundation for retaining valued workers. You can boost your chances of keeping good employees by hiring people for interests, hiring for "microculture," clarifying what you want, and avoiding common hiring traps.

Hire for interests

When you're seeking to fill a vacant position, look for candidates who will feel deeply and passionately *interested* in the kinds of activities that the job in question will entail. People's deep interests in business find expression through eight different "core business interests." The table "Core Business Interests" shows these grouped into three main categories: application of expertise, working with people, and control and influence.

Hiring primarily for interests is far more potent than hiring for skills, values, or even attitude—for several reasons:

- A job that satisfies someone's deepest interests will keep drawing that person's attention and inspiring him or her to perform and achieve.

- A person may be good at a particular job (that is, possess the perfect skills), but if the job doesn't let that individual express core interests, he or she won't be happy with the work for very long.

TABLE 1

Core business interests

Category 1: Application of expertise

Application of technology

Examples:

- Engineering
- Computer programming
- Production and systems planning
- Product and process design
- Process analysis
- Production planning
- Systems analysis
- Mechanical crafting/ manufacturing
- Researching

Theory development and conceptual thinking

Examples:

- Economic-theory developing
- Business-model developing
- Competition analysis
- Designing "big-picture" strategy
- Process designing
- Teaching business theory

Quantitative analysis

Examples:

- Market research
- Forecasting
- Cash-flow analysis
- Computer-model building
- Production scheduling
- Cash-flow and investment analysis
- Accounting

Creative production

Examples:

- New-product designing
- Marketing and advertising
- Developing innovative approaches and solutions
- Event planning
- Conducting public relations
- Entertaining
- Writing
- Illustrating

(continued)

TABLE 1 (continued)

Category 2: Working with people

Counseling and mentoring

Examples:

- Coaching
- Training
- Teaching
- Helping
- Drawing people out
- Supporting
- Providing feedback and advice

Managing people and relationships

Examples:

- Managing others to accomplish business goals
- Directing
- Supervising
- Leading and inspiring others
- Selling
- Negotiating
- Motivating

Category 3: Control and influence

Enterprise control

Examples:

- Controlling resources to actualize a business vision
- Setting strategic direction for a company, business unit, work team, or division
- Having ultimate decision-making authority
- Making deals
- Holding ultimate responsibility for business transactions, such as trades, sales, and so on

Influence through language and ideas

Examples:

- Negotiating
- Deal-making
- Conducting public relations
- Selling
- Persuading
- Designing advertising campaigns
- Communicating ideas through writing or speaking

Note: Often people have more than one interest, so that these categories may overlap. For example, a manager may enjoy working with people *and* applying special quantitative skills.

- It's far easier to help someone to acquire or strengthen skills than to make that person feel enduring passion for his or her work.

Certainly, skills play an important role in matching the right person to the right job. And new hires must have enough of the appropriate background, experience, and abilities to perform well on the job fairly quickly. Nevertheless, a perfect "interests match" will increase the likelihood that the employee will stay with the company more than a perfect "skills match" will.

So, how do you find out what a job candidate's core interests are? Try asking these questions during the interview:

- What have you most loved doing in other jobs?

- What do you like to read? If you're glancing at a newspaper or magazine, what kinds of articles and advertisements are most likely to catch your eye?

- What do you enjoy doing in your spare time?

- What stage of a project really excites you the most?

Then see how his or her responses relate to the categories above. You can also show the candidate the three tables, and ask whether one or more of the eight core business interests seem particularly appealing. Once you've found out where the person's interests lie, you can determine whether those interests are a good fit for the open position.

> *If you want to keep good people, give them as much of*
> *what they want as you can.*
> —Roger E. Herman

Hire for "microculture"

Large and small companies alike have a macroculture—that is, overall ways of doing things, general values, ways of treating and relating to one another, and so forth. They also have several or many microcultures—cultures within the macroculture that characterize different departments, functions, and so on.

For example, to the outside world, a particular organization may seem to have a somewhat formal macroculture, with employees in serious-looking business suits, strict rules of conduct, and so forth. Yet within this same organization, there are likely to be many different microcultures. Perhaps in the software product-design department, long-haired engineers dressed in jeans and sneakers play pranks on each other every day during work breaks. At the same time, just down the hall in the marketing department, professionally coiffed people in precision-pressed business suits stride about with furrowed brows.

Your firm almost certainly has microcultures. The key to hiring right is to *understand* those microcultures—and choose people who will fit into, enjoy, and enrich them. In fact, culture is closely related to *affiliation*—that surprisingly common need to work with people whom we like, respect, and admire. A good "culture match" thus increases your chances of retaining those hard-won new employees.

So, if a job candidate truly enjoys wearing a formal suit to work every day and keeping conversations with colleagues strictly professional, you'll likely want to discourage that candidate from considering a job in a software enclave just down the hall!

*Today's employees are searching for something more
than a paycheck for their work.*
—Jim Harris and Joan Brannick

Clarify what you want

Many hiring decisions start off on the wrong foot because the company hasn't clarified exactly what it wants in the new hire. Often, the different people with whom the new hire will interact (or who have a say in the hiring decision) all have their own ideas about the perfect job candidate. For example, suppose your company wants to fill a product-designer position. In this case:

- The VP of design might want a seasoned individual with extensive design experience gained at one or more of your firm's toughest competitors.

- The head of finance may prefer a bright new (and more affordable) college graduate.

- The marketing director might press for someone who's also picked up some marketing experience with the same kinds of products your company offers.

- The new hire's supervisor may emphasize "people skills" and an ability to work flexible hours—along with all of the above.

To avoid confusion and frustration in evaluating potential hires, try this procedure:

1. Before you even begin interviewing candidates, ask everyone who'll interact with the new hire to *privately* write down exactly what attributes their ideal candidate possesses.

2. Meet to share the various wish lists and openly discuss their differences.

3. Decide together which requirements have priority.

4. Create a new list of requirements that everyone agrees on.

5. *Stick to that list* when evaluating candidates.

Avoid common hiring traps

Don't fall prey to common hiring traps. The first of these is the assumption that your firm has to win the hottest/best/brightest/most sought-after job candidates on the market, with the best grades from the best programs in the best colleges and MBA programs, in order to triumph in the war for talent. That assumption isn't necessarily accurate. In fact, the most sought-after candidates—for example, newly minted, top-of-their-class graduates from the most prestigious business schools—might *not* be your best choice.

Why? Winning them may cost your firm more than it can comfortably afford. Their educational or professional background may be more than what the job in question actually needs. They may be so confident of their desirability that they won't bring a healthy dose of appreciation and gratitude to their new job at *your* firm. And, they'll always have one eye out for the "bigger, better deal."

Some "star" candidates may be worth the above risks. But you might do better if you look for candidates who will feel *honored* to receive a job offer from your firm—people who will appreciate the unique advantages that your organization has to offer. They'll make the most loyal employees. Also, you need to craft a job offer that attracts the people you want and who will best fit with your company.

Another all-too-common hiring trap is looking for people who are just like you. Many managers assume that they can build strong departments or teams by gathering people who all have the same strengths and personalities—those defined by the managers themselves. But remember: Diversity in personality, work styles, and decision-making approaches creates richness in a department's or team's culture. It increases the group's chances of generating creative ideas and solutions. And it lets members complement one another's strengths—and compensate for one another's weaknesses.

Tips for hooking the right prospects

- **Approach each desirable prospect as a unique case.** Work to understand candidates—their interests, needs, and goals— before you first make direct contact with them. Then, frame your offer in a way that hooks them!
- **Make your offer in terms of total compensation**—including base salary, bonus, all forms of equity, and benefits. Add them together, and you can impress the candidate with just how much you're willing to spend to hire him or her!
- **Tell them about opportunities for development and advancement**. Career growth and personal development are important to nearly all job candidates. So be sure to tell them about the training and development programs your company offers; you

can frame them as part of the total compensation package. Talk to them about possible career paths and opportunities for advancement.

- **Help desirable prospects get to know some employees at your company.** One way to do this is to partner candidates with different employees at each meal during onsite visits. By putting prospects in touch with new hires, you allow them to gain a sense of what their own experiences would be like should they join the organization. (Of course, you'll want to choose employees who enjoy meeting new people—and who are positive, "goodwill ambassadors" for the company.)

- **Communicate the quality of your company's culture and environment**—its internal atmosphere—as well as external factors such as the surrounding community, recreational opportunities, and the local school system. Think about inviting a candidate's entire family to visit the area for a weekend.

- **"Sell" your company, emphasizing those aspects most likely to appeal to each individual candidate.** Everyone wants to work for a winner. Your company's reputation, its values and vision, its past record, and its plans for the future are all part of recruiting the right new hires. So "sell" your company, tailoring your pitch to fit individual candidates. For example, with a potential hire who is considering leaving a company in a mature, even stagnant industry, highlight the entrepreneurial aspects of your company and the robust growth of your industry.

Retention Strategy 2: Making Your Company an Employer of Choice

I n addition to hiring right, you can strongly improve retention in your firm by helping to make your company an employer of choice. There are a number of ways to do this. They include designing the right compensation policies, offering attractive benefits, helping employees balance their work and personal lives, fostering employees' self-knowledge, communicating job opportunities, developing employees' talents, creating great jobs, and valuing diversity.

Design the right compensation policies

Compensation is the starting point for any firm that wants to remain competitive in the war for talent. In fact, the single greatest threat you may face is higher salaries offered by other organizations. But here's the good news: Shortfalls in the area of compensation are also the easiest to identify and address.

One strategy is to *figure out what wages your industry is offering.* You can do this by hiring a compensation and benefits consulting firm, tracking classified ads on the Internet, networking with members of human resources organizations, and consulting trade organizations. As another approach, *examine internal pay disparities.* Make sure that the pay for each job is roughly equivalent to that of similar jobs across the organization.

Moreover, *don't assume you have to outspend your competitors.* Just make sure you can meet employees' most important needs. In some industries—for example, information technology—pay *is* king. People can change jobs twice a year and get double-digit percent increases each time. But most people consider other things more crucial or attractive than big pay increases.

Also, remember that salary levels may be the starting point in compensation negotiations, but there are other components to a compensation package. Many people also value things like assistance with personal and professional development, equity or stock options in the company, unusual benefits and perks, a culture that reflects their interests and values, and the chance to work with people they like, respect, and can learn from.

So, even if your firm isn't cash-rich, consider these other options. You can customize creative offerings that may prove more attractive to potential employees than a big paycheck.

Offer attractive benefits

Like compensation, your firm has to provide certain benefits in order to compete in the arena of retention. Today, many companies offer the following basic benefits (in addition to the usual paid vacation and other kinds of leave time):

- Pension and 401(k) plans
- A percentage of employees' health and dental insurance premiums
- A year-end bonus if the company earned a profit in the preceding 12 months
- Stock options
- Onsite or (nearby) offsite child care

- Paid maternity and paternity leave

- Tuition reimbursement

- Membership to a fitness club or an onsite gym

Of course, the kinds of benefits offered vary from culture to culture and across geographic regions. To assess how your company's benefits and perks compare with those of your competitors, apply the same investigative strategies you use to research compensation trends.

As with compensation, even if your firm's benefits and perks don't quite measure up to those of the competition, you can still create an attractive benefits package. With an understanding of employees' needs and interests, along with some creative thinking, your firm can offer special, customized benefits and perks that don't cost much *but* mean a lot to employees. These might include:

- Monthly parties

- A game room

- Onsite massages

- Flex-time

- Nutrition consultations

- Softball league

- Onsite dry cleaning and laundry drop-off

- All-day breakfast bar

- Movie tickets/video library

- Museum passes

- High-tech tools such as smartphones and extra-fast computers

What are the keys to putting together an irresistible benefits and perks program? Creativity, uniqueness, and flexibility. Design creative perks that are individual to your industry. For example, if your company is a bank, you might provide free financial consultation, flexible spending accounts, and mortgage assistance. If your company is a retail clothing-store chain, consider providing free fashion and wardrobe consulting, personal style and color analysis, and the usual merchandise discounts.

Help employees balance their work and personal lives

For many employees, especially single parents or individuals whose spouse or partner also works, the need to maintain a work/life balance—having a home, family, and community life as well as a work life—has become a pivotal issue. Here are some creative ways to meet employees' needs in this area:

- Programs for kids

- A work/life officer or champion within the company

- Paid days off during which employees can volunteer in their communities

- Flexible work arrangements and compressed workweeks

- Job sharing

- Onsite child care

- Teachers who come into work on snow days or vacation days so parents can bring children in rather than miss work

- A lounge for nursing mothers

- A specified number of hours off for employees to attend school appointments or take kids to doctors' appointments

- A "Bring Your Son/Daughter (or Parent!) to Work" day

- A policy stipulating that meetings won't be scheduled before 8 a.m. or after 5 p.m.

Foster employees' self-knowledge

To define and follow their optimal professional path, employees must know themselves—which means being aware of their core business interests, work reward values, and skills. You can help employees strengthen their self-knowledge by giving them access to assessment tools and career and personal counseling.

If your company is small, it may not have a fully appointed career-management center. Still, you can provide employees with periodic onsite or offsite personal and career-development seminars, access to assessment tools through external resources, and sessions with independent career counselors.

If your company does have a career center, ideally it will offer career counselors trained to use assessment tools and counsel employees on the results. At a minimum, it should provide staff with books, CDs/audiocassettes, DVDs/videotapes, and other resources on personal and career development.

Finally, all companies can encourage professional development reviews, during which supervisors help their direct reports clarify their interests, values, skills, and aspirations.

Communicate job opportunities

Many large firms now have online internal job-search tools, or "job banks." But the key to making any job-search tool successful—whether it's an elaborate electronic site serving a large organization or a print binder of open jobs in a small company—is to ensure that the tool describes jobs in terms of:

- The *core business interests* they would let employees express

- The *rewards* they would offer (not just the pay, but also other kinds of rewards, such as affiliation, autonomy, access to state-of-the-art technology, and so forth)

- The *skills* they require (including functional, personal, and technical abilities)

Why is this approach so powerful? For one thing, it helps employees find opportunities that best match their core interests. This matching exerts the strongest influence on how long an employee will stay in a job—and with your company. In addition, it requires the company to think of employees as customers; that is, to clarify—and then meet—their most important and unique needs.

Tips for building an online internal job-search tool and ensuring its success

- **Make sure that the tool's language and presentation convey the message that it's OK to look for a different job within the company**. For example, include a personal note from and photo of the CEO welcoming users to the tool or feature the photos and stories of employees who found new jobs in the company. Message: We care, and we want you to stay with us, whether in your current position or in another.

- **Make the tool fun to use**—perhaps through engaging graphics, interactive exercises, or pithy quotations about work and job-hunting that everyone can relate to.

- **Augment the tool with self-assessment instruments that help employees clarify their interests, values, and skills**—or provide links to self-assessment tools available online.

- **Provide detailed information about jobs in terms of core business interests, rewards, and required skills.** For example: "Of the eight core business interests, these are the two (or three) you'll have the most opportunity to express in this job"; "Of the thirteen rewards you may value, these are the three to five that are the most abundant in this job"; "Of the ten business abilities you have, these are the three to five that are most necessary for success in this job." That way, the employee can "map" his or her self-assessment results directly against each position.

- **Let employees create "personal search agents" (PSAs).** Most online job-search engines allow users to create PSAs that notify them by e-mail whenever a new position matching their interests is posted. Ensure that your internal job-search tool offers similar functionality and have it customized so that employees can specify their core interests, reward values, and skills; preferred locations; full- or part-time employment; and keywords.

- **Publicize the tool and educate employees on how to use it—** through posters, note cubes, workshops, periodic electronic postcards, and so forth.
- **Allow employees to search anonymously.** Some employees will be wary of using their e-mail address in the tool out of a concern that their search will not be confidential. So let them create a nonidentifying e-mail address and use it for searching.
- **Track "hits" per month to see usage patterns and highlight any problems.**
- **Hire an outside technology firm (if necessary) to ensure that the tool accomplishes the above goals.**

Develop employees' skills

Increasingly, companies are identifying the following skills as vital for today's and tomorrow's workplace:

- Technical skills

- The ability to navigate a team-oriented workplace

- An understanding of business ethics

- Time management

- Leadership

- Interpersonal savvy

When you give employees training to develop these skills, you boost the chances that they'll stay with your firm. Why? Because training helps employees perform better and achieve their goals, and people tend to want to stay where they're doing well.

Whether your company is large or small, a start-up or a long-established, international conglomerate, you can support training through resources such as:

- Onsite and offsite workshops

- Seminars

- Courses and other performance-support offerings on your intranet

- Formal and informal mentoring relationships

Tips for using training to foster retention

- **Offer training that gives employees the skills they'll need to keep contributing to the company in the future.** This means thinking ahead to potential trends and changes in your industry, defining the skills and personal abilities that will be important down the road, and helping employees to obtain those skills and abilities.
- **Provide career self-management training to help people chart the best career paths for themselves in your company.** Doing so will encourage them to "think locally" rather than look outside—potentially to your competitors—when they want to make changes.

- **Consider providing educational assistance as a basic benefit.** Supporting employees' continuing education sends the clear message that your firm (like most others) values skills development.
- **Offer continual training in technical skills.** Technical skills go out of date faster than other skills. So make sure that your employees keep their knowledge and skills up-to-date by providing them with ongoing training.
- **Complement technical or task-oriented skills training with training in interpersonal skills.** Not all technically savvy employees necessarily have the interpersonal skills required to perform well in a team-oriented workplace. So in addition to technical training, offer training in interpersonal skills, from basic skills such as how to engage other employees in conversations over lunch, to more challenging skills such as managing emotions, dealing with stress, solving interpersonal problems, and handling conflict.
- **Offer coaching to valued employees who need more help developing their interpersonal skills.** You may see the biggest payoffs from offering personal coaching to high-value employees who lack specific interpersonal skills. Other employees will benefit from group training in maximizing personal effectiveness and eliminating "career Achilles' heels."
- **Familiarize employees with your company's history**—not only in terms of its growth but also in terms of its place in its industry. Knowing the firm's history strengthens employees' sense of their contribution to that history—thus buttressing commitment and loyalty.
- **Communicate your company's vision for the future (its "history of tomorrow today")**—especially if your company is too young to have much of a history, but even if it's not.

- **Communicate statistics to get your CFO's support for investment in training.** If workers get the training they want, 12% of them may still leave their current company anyway. But if they don't get the desired training, 41% will likely leave. In a company of 1,000 employees, the resulting turnover will cost $14.5 million a year.
- **Don't base employees' growth opportunities on their tenure.** Instead, base them on their contributions. This motivates employees to keep improving performance.
- **Encourage managers to identify successors and future leaders, and to inform those star performers of different career paths within the organization**. Together, you and the manager should identify how the company can help them attain their goals.
- **Ask employees to evaluate all training opportunities, and use that feedback to improve your offerings.**

Create great jobs

Another way to help make your company an employer of choice is to offer employees the opportunity to redefine their roles so that their work more closely matches their core interests, reward values, and skills. You can think of this process as "job sculpting," which can occur through regular conversations between managers and their direct reports. During these conversations, both parties use the language of interests, values, and skills to discuss how well a current role suits an employee.

These conversations can take the form of:

- "Stay interviews" or "professional development reviews," during which you ask how employees are doing and clarify what kinds of changes in roles and responsibilities or skills might help improve the match between the job and the individual

- Performance reviews

- Spontaneous meetings requested by the manager or direct report

Several possibilities may come up during these conversations. First, perhaps the employee's current job perfectly matches his or her interests, values, and skills. In this case, you don't need to do anything different.

Second, the current position might mostly suit the employee—but could be even better. In this case, try sculpting to improve the match. For instance, suppose the person would like to do more work related to analyzing quantitative information. In this case, you could suggest that he or she join a special task force assembled to examine market trends in your industry and use the findings to generate ideas for expanding your company's market share.

Third, you may discover that the current role is drastically unsuited to the employee. In this case, you can work with the employee to find a position that better fits his or her interests elsewhere in the company. This boosts your firm's retention "score"—benefiting supervisors, their direct reports, and the company overall.

Value diversity

In many parts of the world today, the workforce is more diverse than ever. From age and gender; to part-time versus full-time status; to ethnicity, race, sexual orientation, and physical ability, companies are benefiting from differences among employees. That's because diverse employees bring a rich array of perspectives, knowledge, and skills that companies can use to solve problems more creatively, enter new markets, and develop fresh offerings.

To attract and keep a highly diverse workforce, you can't rely on "one size fits all" strategies. Instead, you must craft specialized strategies for each major segment of the workforce.

Retaining contingent workers. Members of the "contingent workforce"—part-timers, contractors, and temporary employees—offer some important advantages, as well as difficult challenges, for companies. Primary advantages include flexibility (companies can customize these workers' schedules to meet current work flow and demands, using them only when needed) and affordability (firms save money on payroll taxes, health benefits, and other expenses by employing temps, part-timers, or freelancers).

Challenges include particularly high turnover, which introduces unpredictability and instability into the firm's culture; a lower degree of loyalty to the firm and its products; and a growing demand for the same benefits that regular employees receive—such as satisfying work and career-development support.

Because the contingent workforce is such a valuable resource, many companies are now developing programs designed specifically to retain these employees. To illustrate, in exchange for a work commitment of a specified time, a contract worker may be assigned a "talent agent"—a person who acts as the worker's coach and representative in the company. With the talent agent's help, the worker can cultivate partnerships with other employees. In addition, some companies offer contingent workforce members skills training in exchange for a commitment to work for the firm for a specific length of time.

Retaining younger workers. Younger workers—primarily those in their twenties—bring a special kind of energy, freshness, and state-of-the-art technical knowledge into a firm's workforce. But they pose some difficulties as well. Specifically:

- Demographic trends, in the United States especially, have created an unprecedented shortage of these workers.

- Compared with employees in other age cohorts, young workers are particularly interested in defining their career path and taking jobs that will help them advance to their *next* job.

- Many young workers are more comfortable with rapid change and flat management structures than older employees are. This can create misunderstandings and tensions between generations at work.

- Many younger employees want their employer to define a career ladder for them—a professional track that will let them build up to a level of compensation that will enable them to support starting a family.

To retain your younger workers, apply these strategies:

1. **Understand their background—and customize their work accordingly.** In many economies in which businesses have suffered "downsizing," the younger generation saw their

parents experience job loss, redeployment, and other consequences of shrinking businesses. These young people accept that nothing is certain in the corporate world. Therefore, they're most loyal to their own skills. If there is any group for which job modification or "stretch" assignments (job sculpting) is not only a good but an essential idea, it's this one. At the same time, young people are also comfortable with time-saving and instant-communication devices and so tend to perform tasks quickly (often several at one time). Thus short-deadline, multifaceted projects may be especially appealing to them.

2. **Lead through learning.** Employees in their twenties place a high priority on learning and developing new skills. Provide teaching and coaching on a regular basis, as well as mentoring and internship programs. Give new recruits the opportunity to learn about the rest of the company by allowing employees to make presentations about their departments and jobs.

3. **Seek independent, continuous feedback from them.** Capitalize on this group's everyday learning by soliciting continuous feedback—through face-to-face conversations as well as online tools such as web sites or wikis where employees can exchange insights and ideas for solving problems.

Retaining mature workers. Mature employees (age 50 and up) offer key advantages for companies seeking to define a retention strategy. For example, they bring extensive knowledge and rich business experience—thus embodying a major portion of your firm's intellectual capital. These baby boomers also have the hard-won life skills—such as reliability, patience, or fair-mindedness—that people often gain only by grappling with day-to-day responsibilities over many years.

However, they're all aging together, turning 50 at the rate of about 11,000 per day. So, as they retire in droves, whole plants or departments may be decimated. To keep boomers on your payroll and productive, you may have to create a workplace in which conventional wisdom about job descriptions, hours, pay, benefits, and so on go out the window. Keep these four tips in mind:

1. **Ask your mature workers what they need.** Merely opening a dialogue in this way can help you better serve this age group's needs; for example, many older workers may value long-term health-care insurance more than a big raise.

2. **Support flexibility.** Life seems shorter at 50-plus; many employees at this age want to work part-time, job-share, or telecommute. They're also interested in sabbaticals, unpaid time off, and released time for community projects. Consider any of these offerings, as well as "phased retirement," which lets employees reduce their hours in stages rather than all at once.

3. **Make their work interesting.** On the job, many boomers want autonomy, a sense of meaning, and a chance to keep learning. This can mean redesigning the way tasks get done. Let mature employees work on their own, and provide whatever training they need to pick up new skills—particularly in the area of technology.

4. **Tailor your compensation system.** Avoid "one size fits all" pay plans. For example, while younger employees may want cash,

older ones may prefer larger contributions to a retirement fund. Be creative!

Retaining women. In the United States and many other Western-ized societies, the end of World War II saw an unprecedented flood of women into the workplace. Now, that trend is reversing—in some alarming ways. For instance, women are leaving corporate America at *twice* the rate of men—many of them trading the corporate world for the entrepreneurial frontier.

Why? Many women consider "the glass ceiling" a very real barrier to advancement in the corporate realm. They desire more flexibility. They want to do for themselves what they had previously been doing for employers. Or they've hit on a great idea and identified a market niche, and want to test their business concept in the marketplace.

The resulting "brain drain" carries a heavy price in loss of intellectual capital and damage to staff morale. In addition, it's costly to find replacements for defecting female employees. And, your company may be facing new competition, as many women who leave to found their own business start an enterprise that's directly related to their previous experience.

How can your firm respond? Try these strategies:

1. **Analyze the current situation.** Identify how many women hold upper-management positions in your firm, and how many are in the pipeline. Then talk with these women to find out what's important to them, and then find ways to meet their needs.

2. **Discuss and explore gender-equity issues.** Informal business networks, mentoring opportunities, and after-hours socializing

with clients can help top-notch female managers maintain their career momentum. Gender-awareness workshops can also address both men's and women's concerns, and can provide a common language for discussing gender-related issues.

3. **Eradicate "invisible" barriers to women's success.** Take a hard look at your corporate environment. Barriers to female success can be subtle—but very real. Identify high-potential women and give them equal access to career-enhancing opportunities: line positions, skill-building opportunities, special project assignments, committee leadership, and appointment to high-visibility teams.

4. **Cultivate support throughout the organization.** For example, hold supervisors responsible for meeting the company's gender-equity goals. If your company has an ombudsman to handle any bias incidents, encourage people to use this resource. Send a message signaling acceptance of a broad range of leadership styles.

5. **Promote the understanding that women's ways of managing are good for business.** Many older books on management advise women to act like men in order to succeed. Today, a wealth of research contradicts this approach. Specifically, numerous female entrepreneurs offer more flexibility, understanding, and an open management style—all of which can give their corporations a vital competitive edge. Let female employees who demonstrate these leadership qualities know how much you appreciate them.

Retaining minorities. Members of minority groups defined by race, ethnicity, sexual orientation, physical ability, and other characteristics can further enrich the diversity of ideas, perspectives, and work styles in your company. To retain minorities, consider these approaches:

- **Treat people differently and fairly.** Many people assume that fair treatment means identical treatment. This isn't necessarily true. Sometimes by treating people differently, you're actually treating them more fairly—and helping your company as well. For example, if a valued employee has physical limitations, finding a way to provide him with access to assistive technologies, such as voice-activated software (which isn't something you would do for other employees), might well boost his productivity even further. Both he and your firm benefit.

- **Show your appreciation for diversity.** For example, if your department or team is multicultural or international, initiate workplace social events featuring delicacies from various cultures. These can be fun and educational, and can strengthen bonds among team members.

- **Extract business value from diversity.** For instance, an employee who grew up in a country that your firm does business in might have valuable insights on how businesses operate in that country and what customers might want.

You cannot honor and respect others unless you celebrate the differences between people.
—Beverly Kaye and Sharon Jordan-Evans

Retention Strategy 3: Retaining a Multigenerational Workforce

A generation is a group of people who, based on their age, share a common location in history and the mindset that accompanies it. Demographers have identified the following groups of people most prevalent in today's workforce:

- **The Boomer generation** (born between 1946 and 1964)

- **Generation X** (born between 1965 and 1979)

- **Generation Y** (born between 1980 and 1995)

While it can be problematic to overgeneralize about members of a generation, since unique circumstances shape people as individuals, differences between generations can be traced to the times during which each group came of age.

Research suggests that an individual's most powerful impressions about the world are shaped during adolescence. Thus the common teen experiences of each generation have a profound impact on its members' collective beliefs, behaviors, and assumptions about society and the workplace.

Generations differ in the way they approach work/life balance, loyalty, authority, and other issues that affect your organization. Mastering generational differences will enable you to foster a work environment that appeals to every generation—and retain your top talent.

Different underlying assumptions

Walk around any large organization and you will likely see three generations working side by side. Yet each group has a unique set of underlying assumptions about the work they are doing, and why they are doing it. Generally speaking:

- **Boomers** tend to believe: I want to help change the world—but I also need to compete to win.

- **Generation X** tends to believe: I can't depend on institutions. I need to keep my options open.

- **Generation Y** tends to believe: I need to live life now—and work toward long-term shared goals.

These differing assumptions have significant implications for the role work plays in each generation's lives and what individuals expect to receive from their work.

Boomers at work

Boomers grew up amid general unrest and discontent in many parts of the world. Consequently, many Boomers concluded that the world needed to change—and they felt empowered to get involved. Given the significant size of this population, Boomers also grew up with a lot of other Boomers. Since they frequently had to compete for opportunities throughout their lives, "winning" is very important to them.

These idealistic, cause-orientated, and competitive traits also play out in the workplace. Boomers as a generation are hardworking, are skeptical of positional leaders (even if they hold leadership positions themselves), and prize individual achievement. They also bring:

- Extensive knowledge and rich business experience—they thus embody a major portion of your firm's intellectual capital

- Hard-won life skills—such as reliability, patience, or fair-mindedness—that people often gain only by grappling with day-to-day responsibilities over many years

However, these employees also pose several difficulties for companies:

- They're all aging, turning 50 at the rate of about 11,000 per day. So, as they retire in droves, whole plants or departments may be decimated.

- They can be fiercely competitive, a trait that may not sit well with other generations.

- Many older workers are setting their sights on a second career or a more flexible job opportunity elsewhere.

Strategies for retaining Boomers

To keep Boomers on your payroll *and* productive, you may have to create a workplace in which conventional wisdom about job descriptions, hours, pay, benefits, and the like go out the window. Keep these four tips in mind:

1. **Ask Boomers what they need.** Merely opening a dialogue this way can help you better serve this age group's needs. For example, many older workers may value long-term health care insurance more than a big raise. Also, package new programs and opportunities as a way to "win."

2. **Support flexibility.** Many employees at this age want to work part-time, job-share, or telecommute. They're also interested in sabbaticals, unpaid time off, and time for pursuing opportunities to make a difference, such as engaging in community projects. Consider any of these offerings, as well as "phased retirement," which allows employees to reduce their hours in stages rather than all at once.

3. **Make work interesting and meaningful.** On the job, many Boomers want a sense of meaning and a chance to keep learning, and they want to give back. Employ a variety of reengagement techniques, from fresh assignments to mentoring and knowledge-sharing roles. Also, provide whatever training Boomers need to pick up new skills—particularly in the area of technology.

4. **Tailor your compensation system.** Avoid "one-size-fits-all" pay plans. For example, while younger employees may want cash, older ones may prefer larger contributions to a retirement fund. Be creative!

Generation X at work

Members of Generation X, or Gen Xers, observed financial crises, skyrocketing divorce rates, and rampant unemployment during their teenage years. The first wave of corporate downsizing in the 1980s, in particular, deeply affected their approach to workplace loyalty and contributed to their entrepreneurial spirit.

As a whole, Gen Xers are self-reliant, independent, loyal to their friends, balanced, and adaptable to change. However, they present special challenges for companies seeking to define a retention strategy:

- Demographic trends, in the United States especially, have created an unprecedented shortage of these workers.

- Gen Xers are "free agents" who want to define their own career paths and take jobs that will help them advance to their *next* jobs. They exhibit short-term loyalties and believe that a career is about the individual, not the company.

- This generation knows the rules of the workplace, but its members are inclined to change them to suit their own needs. For them, work/life balance is everything; work must be tailored to fit with other life commitments.

- As Gen Xers at midlife contemplate the next steps in their careers, many feel underappreciated and frustrated by the corporations they work for. Many will consider leaving to start their own businesses or head for nonprofits.

Strategies for retaining Gen X workers

What can your company do to satisfy this critical cohort of leaders as the Boomers head toward retirement? Consider the following strategies:

1. **Earn loyalty by demonstrating commitment.** Gen Xers have learned to accept that nothing is certain in the corporate world. Therefore, they're most loyal to their own skills. Show them that your organization is committed to investing in the skills they'd like to develop. Providing Gen Xers the opportunity to sculpt their jobs to leverage the skills they've acquired will also help retain them for the long term.

2. **Give Gen Xers options for career development.** Gen Xers want to feel that they are in control, and they also want to be heard. Give Gen Xers a variety of choices for their next steps on their career path and ask for their input—it may surprise you. For example, promotions and other specialized responsibilities that appeal to other generations might be exactly what Gen Xers do *not* want. They may see these promotions as limiting their options and skill development.

3. **Re-recruit regularly.** Many Gen Xers continually question whether the job they have today is still the best opportunity possible; thus, they need to be consistently "re-recruited." Recognize their contributions—early and often. Provide stimulating work and let them help solve the company's biggest problems. Flexible work options and the chance to prosper if

the company does are compelling reasons for Gen Xers to stay with your firm.

4. **Provide opportunities for work/life balance.** Gen Xers value time with their family and friends, and appreciate any flexibility that allows them to make this time a priority. Provide this flexibility. Also, minimize moves that sever social connections, such as job relocations.

5. **Set departing employees up to return.** Make sure that the Gen Xers who do leave do so on good terms. Allow them to exit gracefully and keep in touch. They might just come back for the right opportunity.

Generation Y at work

In four years, members of Generation Y (also called Ys or Millennials) will account for nearly half the employees in the world. Tremendous natural disasters and the surge in terrorist violence that Ys saw during their early teen years led them to believe that the world was random and uncertain. As a result, they have an affinity for immediacy and are eager to live in the moment.

These workers also bring state-of-the-art technical knowledge into a firm's workforce; technology and computers have been ubiquitous since their birth. As a group, Ys are upbeat, socially conscious, goal-oriented, and self-confident.

But they pose some difficulties as well:

- Ys have high standards for themselves as well as high expectations of their employers. They expect employers to provide them with a customized road map for achieving success and managers to deliver a near-constant stream of feedback.

- This generation views work as a key part of life, not a separate activity. Ys place a strong emphasis on finding work that's personally fulfilling. If they don't feel that your workplace connects them to a larger purpose, they will take their talent elsewhere.

- Ys' views of time differ from practices in place at most organizations. While they are willing to invest the time required to get the job done, they may chafe at the idea of adhering to a fixed schedule and logging hours at the office for the sake of being present.

- The members of Generation Y are accustomed to a more horizontal and networked world than the hierarchical pyramid that still characterizes most of today's corporations. They are also used to ubiquitous technology and open access to information.

Strategies for retaining Gen Y workers

How can your firm meet its youngest workers' needs and retain the best among them? The following strategies can help:

1. **Make it personal.** Ys expect customized work experiences. They want to be challenged by a range of opportunities, and they have every intention of building their own "perfect" careers. Provide them the growth opportunities they seek,

whether it's conducting a market research project in China or doing a six-month stint in your company's R&D department.

2. **Provide feedback—and expect it in return.** Provide frequent acknowledgment and feedback, enabling Ys to continually learn. Also, solicit feedback on what's working and what's not—through face-to-face conversations as well as online tools. But be prepared for the feedback you receive. Ys are adept at expressing themselves—clearly and often—and they can be blunt.

3. **Think task, not time.** Ys grew up in a world of instant communication (e-mail and text messaging) and tend to perform tasks quickly, often several at one time. Instead of tracking Ys' hours in the office, allow them to work flexibly. Offer Ys opportunities to contribute to short-deadline, multifaceted group projects that play to their strengths.

4. **Emphasize meaning.** Ys' career choices are driven by a desire to play significant roles in meaningful work that helps others. Consider these workers "paid volunteers"—people who join an organization because there's something significant happening there—and provide opportunities for Ys to make a difference.

5. **Lead through learning.** Ys place a high priority on learning and developing new skills. Assign challenging tasks and provide teaching, mentoring, and coaching on a regular basis. Consider innovative practices such as group mentoring, in which a company sets up a technology platform that allows employees to create their own self-organizing groups.

Retention Strategy 4: Cultivating the Right Culture

Many employees cite "culture" as one of the most important reasons for staying with—or leaving—a company. So, it makes sense to take a close look at this sometimes elusive aspect of business.

What is culture?

In the business world, culture derives from:

- **The atmosphere in a company or department:** Is it friendly? Formal? Fast-paced? Methodical?

- **The ways in which people treat one another:** Do they treat each other respectfully? Fairly? Impatiently?

- **The formal and informal guidelines and norms that guide how people do things:** What are the firm's rules about meetings? Where do employees really converse? Who do you really have to go to in order to get something done?

- **A company's true values:** Does it value honesty? Winning the competitive war no matter what?

- **A firm's history:** Were there long years of struggle? Was it an instant success?

- **The nature of an organization's or department's workforce:** Is it diverse? Homogenous?

- Enough other dimensions to make even a seasoned anthropologist's head spin!

Culture is one of those human phenomena that exert an enormous impact on people. Although to a degree culture is intangible, companies can attract and retain valuable employees by being aware of their culture and taking steps to shape it. The process can be challenging—but well worth the effort.

Understand the challenges of cultural change

Shaping a culture can pose several challenges. For one thing, culture is very complex. All companies—even whole industries—have an overall culture, or macroculture. And all but the smallest firms will likely have several microcultures within that larger macroculture. For example, the finance department within a larger company might vary markedly from the product-design department in terms of how it feels to work there, how people treat one another, and so forth.

Culture also has a life of its own. Few people get to actually create a culture (aside from entrepreneurs, perhaps, who are starting up new companies). Instead, culture arises organically as a combination of the many different aspects of a company.

Focus on "microcultures"

Using culture to hire and retain good employees entails knowing and communicating both the macroculture and the appropriate microculture to potential and existing employees. However, it's the *microculture* that plays the most powerful role in people's satisfaction with and enjoyment of their jobs—and thus their likelihood of staying. Your team's or department's microculture is where you have the best chance of understanding and influencing what it's like to work at your firm—and thus make the changes necessary to boost your retention rates.

To focus on microculture, think about what it's like to work in your particular department, division, or team (or in the case of a start-up, the earliest stages of assembling the staff and establishing ways of doing things). To shape that microculture, you'll need to assess its current state, determine the desired state, and make changes needed to close any gaps.

> *A company can only tinker with compensation and benefits.*
> *It's culture, culture, culture.*
> —Norm Snell

Survey your current culture

Take stock of what things are like now in your microculture. You have lots of options for surveying current cultural conditions, including:

- **Informal conversations:** Ask employees what they see as the elements of the culture, and what they like and don't like about it.

- **Formal surveys:** Have employees provide detailed information about the current culture.

- **Direct observation:** Possibly with the help of a consultant, figure out the culture by watching employees' behaviors and considering your own impressions of the department.

Define your desired culture

To find out what kind of culture your employees consider most attractive, try asking them. Through conversations or informal surveys, invite employees to describe their ideal work culture. They might frame their answers in terms like "fun," "cool," "warm," and so forth, or in more specific terms such as "I like to work without getting interrupted" or "I like to have close friends at work."

Also step back and observe. You can glean some ideas about your group's ideal culture simply by watching people and anticipating their needs. For example, suppose most members of your department or team are young, high-energy people who have a habit of working long, intense hours together. In this case, you might reasonably guess they'd appreciate a culture that occasionally lets them rejuvenate and have fun—perhaps through a pizza party every Friday afternoon or a chance to use an onsite game room during breaks.

Make changes to close the gap

There are many ways to close the gap between your current and the desired microculture. In fact, fine-tuning your microculture doesn't have to be difficult. All it takes to cultivate an appropriate culture is a willingness to watch and listen, a little creativity and imagination, and an openness to trying new ideas.

However, remember that employees look at what managers do as well as listening to what they say. If you say, "Let's be casual," but you still wear a suit to work every day, anyone who wants to join your group will probably wear a suit. And if you say, "We care about our people," but focus only on cost control, the culture won't change. That said, by attending to your culture in these ways and really working to change it for the better, you can boost your retention rate dramatically.

Retention Strategy 5: Helping Employees Avoid Burnout

In today's business world, developments such as budget cuts, downsizing, and rapid advances in technology often mean additional responsibilities and overload for employees. For most managers, overload carries with it a serious risk: the burnout and possible defection of their best employees.

The word *burnout* seems to be on everyone's lips these days. But what *is* it exactly? Moreover, what causes it, and why is it such a threat to retention? *Most* important, what can managers do to prevent burnout from worsening attrition—and destabilizing their entire organization?

Understand the warning signs of burnout

Burnout can be defined as *work exhaustion*. Affected employees typically experience these symptoms: lower job satisfaction, eroded commitment to the organization, and higher intention to defect. In some cases, you can see warning signs: an employee seems markedly less confident and exhibits low self-esteem (when there's just too much to be done, some people blame themselves) or the employee expresses a detached or negative approach to colleagues, customers, and clients.

Tips for recognizing the early warning signs of defection

- **Pay attention to a change in behavior.** These include coming in later than usual, leaving earlier than usual, taking breaks out of sight of others, eating lunches alone, dressing more formally than before, or showing major mood changes.
- **Be alert to a decline in performance.**
- **Notice sudden complaints from someone who hasn't typically been a complainer.**
- **Listen for wistful references to other companies or employees who left your firm for another:** "I heard of this guy who got a $20,000 signing bonus!"; "I heard from Sophie, and she's so happy at X. She has her own office, if you can believe that—and she's got a great new product to work on."
- **Watch for a team member who is withdrawing from others—** for instance, someone who has always participated in meetings or volunteered for extra projects is now doing just enough to get by.

Know the root causes of burnout

In a general sense, burnout results from long-term involvement in situations that have too many negatives, such as:

- Work overload

What Would YOU Do?

Retention Through Fairness at BestMed

MICA, A BRAND MANAGER at BestMed, has hired several valuable new group members. In the search process, he took care to clarify the activities required for the new positions, with the result that he found individuals who appear genuinely enthusiastic about performing those activities. Some of these talented new hires are researchers who have come from abroad. The new team is now more culturally diverse than ever.

One day, a native English speaker on the team complains that some of the foreign-born researchers are taking too long to write research reports. All the team members are generating equally high-quality research, but there's some grumbling about "preferential treatment" for the foreign-born researchers "who don't speak English." Mica has even overheard a hallway conversation in which one of the native English speakers mentioned another medical firm that "doesn't have these sorts of problems." He has begun worrying that some of his best employees might defect.

To address the conflict—and control turnover—Mica knows he has to meet all team members' needs fairly. But he wonders how to do that. Should he insist that all team members meet the same deadlines, regardless of their facility with the language? Should he give the foreign-born researchers more time to write the reports, while offering them language training? Should he focus instead on mitigating the emotionally charged discussions of cultural differences, to reduce tensions? He has no idea where to start.

What would YOU do? The mentors will suggest a solution in *What You COULD Do.*

- Conflicting demands ("Do this, but don't neglect that—even for a minute"; "Think big and be creative—but don't make any mistakes.")

- Unclear objectives

- Boredom

- Interpersonal conflict

These same situations usually do not have enough positives to balance them, such as real rewards (bonuses, extra time off, and so on), acknowledgment of employees' contributions, and the sheer joy of scoring successes.

Thus burnout does not stem from just the number of hours an employee is working. A person may work countless hours and still feel motivated. Instead, most people burn out when they feel more stress than support or success in their work life.

Understand the price of burnout

Burnout can directly undermine your company's retention efforts. Why? It's your most highly motivated employees—those who feel a strong commitment to their work—who are most susceptible to burnout. Supervisors can contribute to this problem without even realizing it. Most have a natural tendency to assign critical projects to top performers and then let them handle the workload on their own. And then, when those employees have succeeded with one project, supervisors immediately give them another, without allowing them any time to regroup.

The forces behind burnout can also lead to a vicious cycle that traces and retraces the following steps:

1. In many industries and geographic areas, the "talent pool" shrinks owing to demographic, economic, and workplace changes.

2. As a result, competition for good employees stiffens.

3. Because employees are being courted in creative ways by several different companies, many of them leave their current employers.

4. Some companies become short-staffed as a result.

5. The employees who remain at short-staffed firms are doing the same amount of work that a larger workforce used to handle—and sometimes even more work.

6. They become overwhelmed and leave, putting even more of a burden on remaining employees.

Practice creative staffing

One way to avoid the vicious overload cycle is to create a long-term, strategic staffing plan that ensures there are enough people—and the right people—to do the jobs that need to get done. Here's how:

- Work closely with the human resources department and upper management to define a staffing strategy that will meet your department's and the company's needs. Not all of this will be entirely under your control, but you can help by doing your best to clarify your needs and resources.

- Understand that you may not always be able to get the best person you want for the job—but maybe you can get the second-best, and then bring that person up to speed.

- Figure out ahead of time what your training needs are going to be. That way, you can get new people trained and ready to go as efficiently as possible.

- If your department is especially short-handed and strapped for cash, be strategic about what you ask employees to do. Consider every task in light of whether it adds value for customers. If it doesn't add enough value, eliminate it. (All tasks add some value—be a ruthless judge of just how much.)

- Be willing to redeploy people as needed. Redeployment gives your organization greater flexibility while retaining top employees through times of change and shifting resource needs. Equally important, it gives employees a chance to try "stretch" assignments and gain new experience and skills that may be important to them, as well as to your company.

Tip: In discussing redeployment possibilities with employees, be respectful of employees' thoughts and feelings. Rather than moving employees around like chess pieces, think about what might make the best reassignment opportunities for them—and emphasize any professional-development benefits offered by those opportunities. Redeployment should be optional for employees. If a reassignment does take place, check with redeployed personnel to see how things are going, and devise solutions to any problems that arise.

Steps for managing exhausted employees

1. **Talk with employees who are complaining of impending burnout to determine whether work exhaustion is causing the problem.** Talking can help you determine whether the complaints are stemming from work exhaustion. Without asking, it's difficult to distinguish between work-exhaustion causes, or other causes such as personal strain, health problems, or family concerns. For example, listen for comments like the following, which all signal work exhaustion:
   - "I have way too much to do—I can't keep up with it all."
   - "The more I do, the more work I get."

- "I'm trying to do everything perfectly, and I just can't manage."
- "Upper management's changing priorities around way too fast—it's confusing."
- "We don't have enough help around here."
- "They keep raising the bar but don't give us the resources we need to get the job done."

2. **If the cause of the impending burnout is work exhaustion, figure out whether the employee attributes the exhaustion to a personal weakness or deficiency, or to reasons external to him- or herself.** An employee's attribution of the cause for a negative situation can inform your decisions about how to ease the problem. Does he or she see an external force as responsible? ("It's my manager's/the customers' fault.") Or does the employee assign responsibility to him- or herself for the situation? ("I guess I just haven't learned to manage my time well enough to keep up.")

3. **Determine whether the employee believes that something can be done to improve the situation.** When employees believe that nothing can be done to ease their overload, they're more likely to seriously consider leaving the company—or, perhaps even worse for all concerned, to stay but fall into a depressed state of "malaise" (what psychologists call "learned helplessness"). If they think that hope is in sight, they're more likely to consider staying and seeing whether things actually improve. Discerning which belief an employee holds lets you decide how much encouragement or reassurance to give, and shapes what you do next.

4. **Develop an action plan with the employee.** As you work with the employee to shape an action plan to solve the crisis, keep in

mind whether the employee attributes the cause of his or her overload to internal or external factors. For example, if the employee admits to being so much of a perfectionist that he or she can't manage the workload, try these steps:

- Clarify expectations or target dates.
- Point out that the person is carrying an unusually large load and doesn't need to do everything perfectly.
- Carefully explain that the person is working toward unrealistic standards compared with most other employees.

If the employee attributes the overload to external factors, let him or her know that you will work on:

- Improving methods of assigning tasks
- Developing realistic expectations
- Adding resources
- Providing needed training

5. **Periodically evaluate your action plan.** That way, you and your employees can determine whether the actions taken are eliminating the causes of the exhaustion.

Minimize work exhaustion

Here are some suggestions for minimizing work exhaustion:

- Be aware of the issue. Understand the nature of work exhaustion, its impact on employees and the organization, and the vulnerability of top employees.

- Monitor workloads and morale, especially among your top performers. Consciously identify your best people and meet with them regularly to see how they're doing. This act alone can help people feel supported—which can tip the balance between negatives and positives in their work.

- Be aware of who your "hero" managers are—those managers who consistently try to do too much and push too hard. Help them to stop burning out their employees—and themselves.

- Show your appreciation for valued workers. This, too, can help outweigh some of the other negatives.

- Consider redesigning some jobs. Often, jobs evolve into "no-win" situations without anyone being aware of it. Recognize when this is happening, and brainstorm with employees ways to reshape their roles before burnout strikes.

- Manage exhausted employees by acknowledging cries for help—such as "I don't know how to keep up" or "Looks like I'm going to have to work over the weekend again." Talk with the employee about the problem, generate ideas for alleviating the situation, and develop an action plan for change.

"Re-recruit" your top talent

Don't fall into the all-too-common trap of taking valued employees for granted or assuming that, because they work for you now, they'll want to keep working for you. Instead, assume that you need to consistently "re-recruit" them.

Decide which one-third of your people are your top performers. Then remind yourself often that these individuals are the ones who are always being recruited by your firm's competitors. Frequently show your best people how much you appreciate them—whether it's through informal and heartfelt thanks for a job well done, small but meaningful tokens of appreciation such as notes or flowers or tickets to an event, or more substantial thanks in the form of a bonus or extra "comp time."

Meet with them on a regular basis to find out how they feel about their jobs. If you sense dissatisfaction, ask your stars to clarify why they're unhappy and explore opportunities for improving the situation within their job and the company. Devise a solution. Here are some examples:

- If the problem has to do with the relationship between you and a direct report—for instance, difficulties with communication or with performance expectations—regular meetings to address the issues often help. Getting assistance from your human resource specialist could also improve the situation.

- If the concern is wages, perhaps you can support giving the person a raise. Firms typically analyze compensation within their industry, which your human resource specialist (if your company has one) can share with you. Try to problem-solve to provide other intangible benefits that will have meaning and value in addition to straight compensation. Such benefits might include training in new skills, which has both monetary and development value.

- If a high performer is complaining about a lack of affinity in the department, consider how you can build community within your work group. You could sponsor functions or events that give employees time to build these personal networks and have fun, such as joining a company baseball team.

- If star employees want to leave because their work no longer interests them, find ways to modify their current roles to better match their interests or help them identify more satisfying opportunities within the company. It may be painful for your department to lose them, but by keeping them in your organization, you help the firm to continue benefiting from their talents.

What You COULD Do.

Remember Mica's concern about how best to handle the possibility of employee defections in his culturally diverse team?

Here's what the mentors suggest:

In managing performance and retention in a culturally diverse group, many managers assume that fair treatment means identical treatment. But sometimes treating people fairly means treating them differently. By giving foreign-born researchers more time initially to do their work and providing them with training to strengthen their writing skills, Mica may appear to be treating them unequally. But he would actually be giving all the researchers *equal opportunity* to succeed. With support and success, talented researchers will be more likely to stay at BestMed—improving retention in the organization and enabling BestMed to benefit from the diverse perspectives, experiences, and knowledge they bring.

Retention
Strategy 6:
Strengthening Your
Retention Skills

B y strengthening your overall retention skills, you can further help your company keep valued employees on board even in a highly competitive labor market. Keys include taking advantage of retention training, sharing lessons learned with peer managers, and taking steps to become a "retention champ" as well as reward champs in your group.

Take advantage of retention training

Clearly, retaining valued employees takes some skill and practice. Few managers know all the skills required to increase retention. To strengthen managers' retention abilities, many firms offer workshops, seminars, and other learning opportunities that focus on how to attract and keep valued employees. If your company offers such training programs, take advantage of them. The investment of your time will pay big dividends.

These learning opportunities are valuable because they often address the following aspects of retention:

- Seeing employees as customers (yes, you are "buying" their time, but they are also "buying" your job!) and human beings with full lives, not just as parts in a machine.

- Speaking the language of core business interests, reward values, and skills.

- Proactively asking the right questions and making observations in order to assess cultural conditions and employee "fit" within those conditions.

- Being sensitive to diversity issues.

- Detecting early signs of dissatisfaction and possible defection.

- Understanding what really makes people stay in a job and what really makes them leave.

- Understanding the true costs of attrition—including eventual loss of customers.

If your organization doesn't have this kind of training and support available, ask for it. Everyone will benefit.

> *Managers and supervisors have the most critical role to play in winning the race of talent.*
> —Beverly Kaye and Sharon Jordan-Evans

Share lessons learned with peer managers

Keeping valued employees requires a complex mix of learnable skills, gut-level intuition, and sensitivity. But you don't have to struggle alone with this. You can share your experiences with retention and lessons learned with other managers. By exchanging stories about successes *and* failures—informally or through periodic meetings—you can help one another avoid typical mistakes and obstacles as well as build on each other's knowledge and wisdom. You can also monitor how well others' retention rates are meeting the firm's goals and lend one another moral support.

Become a retention champ

To become a retention champ, make sure you understand your company's retention target rates for positions in your department or group. Also show that you are free from "parochial" interest—the narrow perspective that arises when managers try to keep high performers even though those employees would be happier and more productive by moving to a different position in the organization. In other words, demonstrate that you're willing to help good employees leave their groups for another job in the company, rather than trying to hold them back, only to see them go to another firm.

Finally, help all the team leaders and supervisors in your group become retention champs, too. Encourage them to learn about retention and to demonstrate all the skills associated with it. Reward them for using retention strategies to keep valued employees in their teams or in the company overall.

Steps for diagnosing and closing retention gaps

1. **Collect and analyze all employee turnover and exit-interview data.** Remember: Exit-interview information is valid only if the departing employee trusts the interviewer. When conducting an exit interview, make absolutely certain the employee knows

that the interview contents will remain confidential. And with each departure, list and add up the various costs of losing that individual. Use that list as a starting point for defining retention goals, and add to it as employees leave and new hires come on board. For example, in assessing turnover costs, don't forget often-overlooked costs such as loss of company and industry knowledge, stress on employees picking up the slack, moving allowances for new employees, disgruntled customers, and loss of other employees through the all-too-common domino effect.

2. **Survey managers to get their attitudes about and experiences with retention.** Again, the assurance of confidentiality is essential to get honest answers. Be sure to survey managers at all levels. Then, compare midlevel managers' responses to those of supervisors and senior leaders. For example, different managers may have different ideas about what retention rates in their groups should be. The head of the sales department may not be as concerned about retention as the IT manager is.

3. **Look ahead in a "future pull" session.** Imagine that, one year from now, your senior team is celebrating its retention for that year. What would you like to see? Brainstorm possible scenarios, and write them down. Then back up from the outcomes and brainstorm the scenarios that went into bringing about those outcomes. For example: "We've retained 95% of our top talent"; "Good people are banging at our doors"; "Customer retention rates have increased 10%."

4. **Identify the "pain points" created by weak retention.** Include numbers and costs wherever possible. For example: "We lose 15% of our talent every year"; "We're constantly orienting and

training replacements"; "An employee who left last year took a key customer, and we lost a $50,000 contract."

5. **Identify obstacles to achieving the desired future state you defined in Step 3.** For example, perhaps managers are ill-equipped to improve retention, the organization lacks a retention mind-set, or the organization doesn't offer career-development resources to employees.

6. **Brainstorm potential strategies for closing the gap.** Review the retention strategies suggested in this topic and adapt them to your organization and the particular challenges you're facing.

7. **Gather input and insights from focus groups and interviews.** Use the "future pull" process with focus groups representing multiple levels and functions in the organization—the diverse and numerous stakeholders. For example, ask group members:
   – What they feel is unique about your retention situation
   – What is working for you and against you in trying to meet your retention goals
   – Why they think people stay
   – Why people leave, and what attrition costs the organization
   – What could be done to lessen attrition
   – What keeps them at the company

8. **Use the information you've collected to develop a set of retention strategies and goals for the company.** Use all the information from the above steps to give senior managers feedback and present recommendations such as the following:
   – Develop a consistent strategic retention plan for the organization.
   – Emphasize the importance of retention to all managers, supervisors, and team leaders.

- Put support structures in place—for example, a retention champion or task force.

9. **Tap a retention champion.** Place someone in charge of designing ongoing retention strategies. Let this person interface as much as possible with recruiters, coaches, trainers, line managers, and individual contributors. Consider appointing rotating retention champions in all departments.

10. **Organize a retention task force.** Get internal help from a diverse group of managers and employees who can monitor turnover situations and work together to address them. Be sure the group has enough time and resources reserved for them to manage their ongoing charge.

Tips and Tools

Tools for Retaining Employees

CONDUCTING A "STAY INTERVIEW"

You're no doubt familiar with "exit interviews," conducted when people are leaving positions. This worksheet is for a "stay interview," which you conduct before people even consider leaving, to help you learn what you can do to avoid having to conduct an exit interview.

What interests you the most? (This question encourages employees to think about their core interests. You can then talk together about how well their current role lets them express their core interests.)

What motivates you? (This question gets at work reward values. For an increasing number of employees, factors other than a big paycheck are important—especially in economic boom times, when a healthy pay stub is readily available. Note: *Don't* assume that your employees value the same work rewards that *you* do.)
Example: If you learn that an employee puts family life first, offering flex-time may earn his loyalty. Another employee may crave a sabbatical to do volunteer work in her community.

What do you do best? (This question helps employees assess their skills. You can then talk together about how well their current roles match their skills or provide opportunities for them to "stretch." Then you can define any necessary skill-development efforts.)

What are your short-term goals? (During an interview, see how these objectives fit with a current job opening. Over time, keep an eye on how they change—so you can help the employee keep improving. By monitoring changes in goals, you can sense what kind of employee you've got: driven, steadfast, creative, and so forth.)

What are your long-term goals? (If the answer requires skills your employees don't have, suggest appropriate training or "stretch" opportunities.)

How do your short-term goals fit your long-term goals? (The first time you ask this one, the employee may not have an answer. But the question prompts people to start *thinking* about how to get from point A to point B—which is good for their careers and useful in their current responsibilities.)

What do you need from me? How can I—or the company—help? (Asking this question is a powerful move. It shows employees that you're interested in their future and their personal development, and it gives you the information you need to manage them well.)

CALCULATING THE COST OF REPLACING A SPECIFIC EMPLOYEE

Use this form to calculate the cost of employee turnover in one position or salary range per year. Calculate costs for replacement employees only. Do not calculate costs for employees hired to fill new positions.

Position:	Salary level:

Hiring costs

Direct costs to hire 1 new employee

Advertising	
Average fee to employment agencies, placement firm	
Sign-on bonus	
Referral bonus to current employees	
Travel and expenses (include yours and money you reimburse to prospective candidate)	
Other direct costs	
Total direct costs to hire	

Indirect costs to hire 1 new employee

Estimate the costs incurred by having all *current employees perform the following activities related to a new hire:*

Interviewing (costs of current employees at all levels of interviewing, from initial phone call through final interviews)	
Checking references	
Lost revenue (include costs of time spent away from actual jobs)	
Miscellaneous indirect costs (phone, copy, fax)	
Total indirect costs to hire	

Training costs	
Direct costs to train 1 new employee	
Time spent by person/people directly responsible for training new hire to do job. Cost per hour times number of hours.	
Cost per participant of general training programs, training materials, seminars for new hires	
Travel and expenses per participant for above	
Other direct costs	
Total direct costs to train	
Indirect costs to train 1 new employee	
Estimate the time spent by all *current employees who are involved in training a new candidate:*	
General training in company technology and procedures, processes, etc.	
On-the-job training costs before employee becomes fully productive	
Total indirect costs to train	
Estimated revenue lost by vacant position	
Total Costs: Single Employee	
Annual cost of employee turnover	
To calculate the annual cost of employee turnover, multiply the cost of replacing one employee times the number of replacements each year.	

WORK CULTURE SURVEY

Use this tool to help you, your team, or your work group assess the group's microculture within the larger organization. This can help you hire new employees who will thrive in this type of culture, and also identify ways to better meet current employees' needs and expectations.

Our current work atmosphere

How informed and involved do I/we feel in our group's overall strategy and decision making?

☐ Very ☐ Not at all

How do we dress for work?

☐ Formally ☐ Casually ☐ Mixed

How much spontaneous gathering for fun, breaks, and stress relief do we engage in?

☐ None ☐ Some ☐ A lot

How much do we get together outside of the office?

☐ None ☐ Some ☐ A lot

How much privacy and quiet do I/we have?

☐ None ☐ Some ☐ A lot

What kinds of *overall* culture do I/we think our group emphasizes? *Check as many as apply.*

☐ **Customer service** (emphasizing creating internal and/or external customer solutions and getting close to customers by anticipating their needs and creating value for them)

☐ **Innovation** (emphasizing new ideas, processes and products, taking risks, embracing change, and so forth)

☐ **Operational excellence** (emphasizing efficiency, effectiveness, smooth operations)

☐ **Spirit** (emphasizing creating environments that inspire employee excellence and creativity, lift people's spirits, unleash energy and enthusiasm, and focus on striving toward a greater common goal)

Does our group's culture have enough "give" in it to accommodate different kinds of people, or is it a "love it or leave it" affair? (Be honest!)

More specifically, what parts of the culture does someone *have* to subscribe to in order to fit in?

Other important things about our culture (values, unspoken rules, etc.):

Ideas for improving the culture
Are there any important gaps between what kind of atmosphere you would like to work in and what kind of atmosphere currently characterizes our group? If so, what are they?
What measures might help improve our work culture and/or help close gaps between what we want or need and what exists?

RETENTION SELF-ASSESSMENT

Use this self-assessment to help you get a sense of how your attitudes and behaviors as a manager might influence retention in your department. Check either Yes or No for each of the 15 questions below, then see the instructions for interpreting your results.

Do you ...	Yes	No
1. ... believe that managers can play an important role in their firms' retention rates?		
2. ... regularly hold "stay interviews," professional development reviews, or other meetings in which you and your employees discuss how they're doing?		
3. ... have a clear sense of your department's, division's, or team's microculture and how well it suits the majority of your people?		
4. ... think that employees' family and personal lives are just as important as their work lives?		
5. ... join in the fun when others are taking breaks, sharing jokes, and generally relieving stress?		
6. ... make an effort to listen for, understand, and address the unique concerns or needs of the diverse employees in your group?		
7. ... understand each employee's core business interests, work reward values, and skills—and how well his or her current role suits all three?		
8. ... have a strategy in place for detecting and addressing potential burnout among your team?		
9. ... know exactly how much turnover in your group costs the company—in terms of dollars?		
10. ... believe that most employees don't consider compensation the most important aspect of their work?		
11. ... feel comfortable with the idea of "job sculpting" (redefining an employee's current role so that it better matches his or her core interests) and helping employees find other opportunities within the company if sufficient sculpting isn't possible?		

12. . . . think that employees' personal and professional development is important to them and find ways to support them in this effort?		
13. . . . have clear retention targets established for each function and role in your department and have a process in place for assessing how well you're meeting those targets and closing any gaps?		
14. . . . routinely acknowledge your people's contributions in personal, creative ways?		
15. . . . know exactly which of your people are your top one-third performers and which are your high-potential people?		
Score		

Interpreting your score: *If your Yes's outnumber your No's, you're on the right retention track. If your No's far outnumber your Yes's, skim the Core Concepts in this topic again to get more familiar with retention issues and strategies.*

Test Yourself

This section offers ten multiple-choice questions to help you identify your baseline knowledge of the essentials of Retaining Employees.

Answers to the questions are given at the end of the test.

1. Retention is:

a. Keeping all employees as long as you possibly can.

b. Keeping talented employees for an appropriate length of time.

c. Keeping only those employees who enjoy the company's culture.

2. True or false: Most people leave their jobs because they're not getting paid enough or they find the company's benefits package unsatisfactory.

a. True.

b. False.

3. Why is keeping valued employees especially important in today's atmosphere of intensifying business competition?

a. It protects your firm from being investigated for questionable hiring practices, union policies, and employee discrimination.

b. Retention ensures that you'll keep the most desirable employees in the overall talent pool longer than any of your competitors and that you'll find those employees that best match your firm's overall macroculture.

c. Intellectual capital (which people possess) is becoming more important to companies' competitiveness, the costs associated with employee turnover are increasing, and retention has a powerful impact on customer satisfaction and profitability.

4. Which of the following does *not* constitute a reason that retention is so challenging for some companies these days?

a. In some geographic regions, the overall workforce is maturing while birthrates have been declining.

b. More and more workers have inherited enough money from previous generations and can expect healthy early-retirement benefits from Social Security so that they don't need to work as much as preceding generations had to.

c. In some geographic regions, unemployment rates are falling and the economy is booming. Thus companies are spending more and more of their resources to attract fewer and fewer available workers.

5. Kenneth Takahara is human resources manager of TraqDown Systems Inc., a developer of high-tech navigation equipment. His staff is a mix of Generation Y workers and a smaller number of Boomer employees in key positions. Kenneth develops a list of strategies designed to meet the needs of his employees and maximize retention. Which strategy is most likely to appeal to the Boomers in his group?

a. Introduce more flexible work opportunities, such as job sharing, sabbaticals, and telecommuting.

b. Provide opportunities to contribute to a wide variety of short-deadline, multifaceted group projects.

c. Set up a series of in-house seminars focused on key business skills, such as negotiation, making presentations, and project management.

6. Which of the following hiring strategies is *not* necessarily a way to improve retention?

a. Hiring people who will feel deeply and passionately interested in the activities that the job will entail.

b. Hiring people who are the best and most sought-after candidates on the job market.

c. Hiring people who best match your department's or division's microculture.

7. Which of the following is uppermost in most employees' minds today and therefore the most important way for your firm to attract and retain the best employees?

a. Compensation.

b. Benefits and perks.

c. Personal and professional development.

8. Which of the following statements is *not* true about a company's or department's culture?

   a. The atmosphere and the ways in which people treat each other can strongly influence culture.

   b. It's more important to match employees to your department's culture than to your company's culture.

   c. Many employees think of "culture" as one of the least important reasons for staying with—or leaving—a company.

9. True or false: The most effective way to keep an employee from leaving who has just given notice is to counteroffer with a larger salary than his or her potential new employer is offering.

   a. True.

   b. False.

10. The best way to help employees avoid burnout is to:

   a. Create a long-term, strategic staffing plan that ensures that there are enough people—and the right people— to get needed work done, and help employees manage workloads.

   b. Provide plenty of punching bags, boxing gloves, and other stress-relief "toys" around the office.

   c. Require all employees to use up their vacation time on a regular, structured basis.

Answers to test questions

1, b. Sometimes it's perfectly appropriate and beneficial for both the company and the individual if an employee moves on to a different firm after working for a specific amount of time for your company. This can be especially true for entry-level high-tech positions. By having young workers move on after a few years, you can refresh your talent pool with more up-to-date workers who possess the latest high-tech experience and education.

2, b. It's actually a myth that pay and benefits most drive job satisfaction and keep people at a company. In fact, most people look for other kinds of things in their work: a supportive supervisor, satisfying work that lets them express their deepest interests, and rewards that mean the most to them—such as challenging assignments, access to state-of-the-art technology, and other nonmonetary motivations.

3, c. These three trends are changing the business landscape so that keeping valued employees now gives your firm its sharpest competitive edge.

4, b. More workers are not in fact inheriting enough money to be able to work less than preceding generations. Thus, this is not a primary reason that retention has become especially challenging for some companies today.

5, a. Supporting job flexibility is a more effective strategy for retaining Boomers. Older workers are also interested in unpaid time off and time for community projects. Consider any of these offerings, as well as "phased retirement," for Boomers.

6, b. Hiring the "hottest" prospects may not help you improve retention. These individuals may be so confident of their desirability that they won't bring a healthy dose of appreciation and gratitude to their new job at *your* firm. Consequently, they'll always have one eye out for the "bigger, better deal."

7, c. Many employees today are most concerned with managing their own personal development and careers—and getting support in this effort from their employers. In fact, offering employee-development support may make your firm more attractive to potential and current hires than a big paycheck or hefty benefits.

8, c. Many employees actually cite "culture" as one of the *most*, not least, important reasons for staying with or leaving a company. Therefore, you can improve retention by being aware of your department's culture and taking steps to shape it so that valued employees embrace it.

9, b. Counteroffering is a common response when an employee gives notice—but it's not the wisest. That's because it doesn't get to the root of why most employees leave. Often, they're leaving because they're not happy with their supervisor, their work, or the company itself. Counteroffering may tempt them to stay—but the same old problems will soon crop up again, prompting further attempts to find a job outside the company.

10, a. Strategic staffing and wise management of employees' workloads can stave off the feelings of hopelessness that can cause overburdened employees to leave.

FAQs

Since it costs so much to lose and replace employees, shouldn't my firm try to keep everyone for as long as possible?

Not necessarily. Poor performers can hurt morale, so you should not invest in retaining them beyond trying to help them improve. Also, sometimes it's better for both an employee and your firm if an individual moves on after a few years (for example, in a function that requires just short-term time commitments).

What exactly is intellectual capital?

It's the unique knowledge and skills that the employees who make up a company's workforce possess. Examples include computer programmers who know the latest programming languages, direct-marketing analysts who understand the most recent marketing trends in your company's industry, top managers who possess broad experience in understanding and motivating people, the administrative assistant who knows just whom to call to get this done or that started, and so forth.

Is retention equally difficult for all companies these days?

No—it's relative and depends on factors such as industry characteristics, cultural expectations, and economic and demographic trends. Retention patterns can vary by geographic region, and can change from decade to decade within the same country. In some cultures, employees who leave their companies are looked on with suspicion (lifelong employment and mutual loyalty are the norm), so retention is not considered a challenge.

If my firm has a highly diverse workforce, should I treat everyone the same in order to be as fair as possible?

Not necessarily. Fair treatment doesn't automatically mean equal treatment. To improve retention in a diverse workforce, you need to listen to and meet each group's special needs and concerns in order to keep your best performers. For example, suppose you've got a talented employee who has physical limitations. You could improve your chances of keeping him by providing him with assistive technology (for example, voice-activated software) that you may not provide to other employees. This is unequal treatment—but it's fair. And it benefits both the employee and your firm.

I understand that hiring right is the first step to retention. What can I do to hook the hottest, most sought-after recruits from the best schools?

Well, before you start, think about whether those individuals are necessarily the right prospects for your firm. Newly minted, top-of-their-class graduates from the most prestigious business schools, for example, may cost more than your firm can afford. Moreover, their educational or professional background may be more than what the job in question actually requires. But equally important, they may be so confident of their desirability that they won't really appreciate their new job at your firm—and they'll always have an eye out for the "bigger, better deal." It's smarter to match a prospect's cost, qualifications, and attitude to your firm's particular situation and needs instead of automatically reaching for the most sought-after recruits.

Business has been healthy lately for my company, so whenever someone gives their notice, we make the person an impressive counteroffer that beats the salary the other firm is offering. But many of these people end up leaving after a while anyway. What's going on?

The problem is that, while it's important that your compensation practices remain competitive, compensation is not always the main reason people leave their jobs. Other important reasons include unhappiness with an immediate supervisor relationship, dissatisfaction or boredom with work responsibilities, lack of opportunities to develop personally and professionally, and other nonmonetary concerns. By making a counteroffer of a higher salary, you're in effect revealing to that person that you don't understand his or her real reasons for wanting to leave. A big raise might tempt the individual to stay for a time, but eventually he or she will give notice again if those real reasons for the dissatisfaction remain unaddressed.

I hear so many stories about companies' offering employees high-priced cars, week-long trips to expensive spas, and other fancy

perks in order to hold onto workers. How can I keep employees if my firm can't afford those kinds of perks?

You don't need to spend a lot of money to attract and keep good employees. To the contrary, what you need to do is to identify what matters most to them and then provide perks that will meet those needs in tailored, creative, and affordable ways. For example, design creative perks that are unique to your industry. If your company is a bank, you could provide free financial consultation, flexible spending accounts, and mortgage assistance. Or if you're a retail clothing-store chain, offer free fashion and wardrobe consulting, and personal-style and color analysis. The possibilities are virtually endless. But the best way to keep employees today is still through good, old-fashioned support of their personal and professional development—through training, seminars, a well-stocked and staffed career center, and other relatively affordable resources.

I'm a manager at a large company. We pride ourselves on understanding our overall culture and hiring people who fit into it. But this doesn't seem to be enough to keep those new hires. What are we doing wrong?

A large company's overall culture is certainly important, but microculture—the atmosphere, values, and so on, in an individual division, department, or team—plays a much more crucial role in retention. Microcultures can vary dramatically within one corporation. For instance, your product-development group might consist primarily of informal, creative, fun-loving employees who tease each other and like to dress casually, while just down the hall, the marketing staff might stride around in severe-looking business suits, with serious looks on their faces. New employees are going to be spending most of their time within those microcultures. Therefore, understanding and fine-tuning microcultures gives you your best opportunity to attract and retain the most appropriate employees. The key is to find out (through surveys or direct observation) what kind of culture most of the employees within a microculture are looking for, assess the current situation, and devise strategies for closing any gaps.

At my firm, we've started taking exit interviews very seriously in an effort to improve our retention rates. But we haven't seen significant improvements in our rates yet. Why?

Exit interviews can yield some important information. However, in most exit interviews, companies just scratch the surface of why employees are leaving. Why? During the interviews, employees mostly report on what's attractive about their new job—without explaining the real reasons they were looking for new work in the first place. So, you're getting incomplete information that is not sufficient for you to make the kinds of changes necessary to improve retention rates—before employees give notice. Exit interviews are helpful, but they're like employment postmortems. You'll usually get better data from patients (that is, your current employees) who can—and will—talk about their symptoms.

My firm just established a retention task force. What can we do to help our managers and supervisors improve retention in their various departments?

Here are three things you can do: (1) offer workshops and other training that shows managers how to match job responsibilities to employees' core business interests, work reward values, and skills; (2) provide managers with avenues (informal conversations or regular meetings) in which to share and learn from one another's experiences with retention; and (3) recognize and reward retention champs by establishing clear retention targets for each function, tying compensation to retention rates, and discouraging "parochial" interest (managers' efforts to keep high performers even though those employees would be happier elsewhere in the organization).

What can I do to keep my best performers from experiencing burnout—and leaving?

Think about how you may be inadvertently contributing to work exhaustion among your top people. Do you tend to be a hero—someone who's always trying to do too much and pushing yourself and others too hard? For example, you probably give the most challenging work to your best people (makes sense, right?) and then trust that they'll handle it themselves (after all, they've proven that they don't need close supervision, right?). Take time to regularly ask people how they're doing. If you hear or see signs of exhaustion (changes in work habits, health, or personality; comments like "Whew, I don't know if

I can keep up"), determine the source of the exhaustion. Some employees blame themselves; others blame external sources such as conflicting priorities from supervisors, unclear goals, and so forth. Once you determine the source, you can take appropriate action—by helping employees set more realistic standards for themselves, or by clarifying your department's or team's goals and priorities.

Key Terms

Affiliation. The opportunity to work with liked, admired, and respected colleagues; a work reward value that many employees consider important.

Attrition. The departure of employees.

Burnout. Work exhaustion resulting from overload or other changes in an employee's work situation.

Demographic change. Change in the makeup of a population (for example, age, gender, or racial proportions, and so on).

Diversity. Variation in age, gender, race, ethnicity, sexual orientation, physical ability, and other characteristics in the workforce.

Free agency. Self-employment, in which workers serve various clients on a temporary, contractual basis.

Intellectual capital. The knowledge and skills that employees possess.

Job sculpting. Reshaping an employee's current role so that it lets the person express his or her core business interests, get the work rewards he or she values most, and use or learn the skills that the individual wants to develop.

Macroculture. A company's overall atmosphere, values, and ways in which people treat one another.

Microculture. A division's, department's, or team's atmosphere, values, and ways in which people treat one another.

Retention. A company's ability to keep talented and valued employees who will help their organization remain competitive.

Turnover. The change in a company's workforce as employees leave and new hires arrive.

Work/life balance. The opportunity for employees to devote adequate time to both work and nonwork matters in their lives.

To Learn More

Articles

Butler, Timothy and James Waldroop. "Job Sculpting: The Art of Retaining Your Best People." *Harvard Business Review* OnPoint Enhanced Edition. Boston: Harvard Business School Publishing, September–October 1999.

> This white paper offers stunning statistics on current retention trends and demographic changes, as well as a wealth of advice on how companies can recruit and retain the best employees for them.

Cappelli, Peter. "A Market-Driven Approach to Retaining Talent." *Harvard Business Review* OnPoint Enhanced Edition. Boston: Harvard Business School Publishing, March 2001.

> Open competition for other companies' people, once a rarity in business, is now an accepted fact. Fast-moving markets require fast-moving organizations that are continually refreshed with new talent. But no one likes to see talent leave; when a good employee walks, the business takes a hit. It's futile to hope that by tinkering with compensation, career paths, and training efforts, you can wall off your company from today's labor market. But there is an alternative: a market-driven approach to retention based on the assumption that long-

term, across-the-board loyalty is neither possible nor desirable. By taking a hard look at which employees you need to retain and for how long, you can use highly targeted programs to keep the required talent in place.

Field, Anne and Ken Gordon. "Do Your Stars See a Reason to Stay?" *Harvard Management Update,* May 2008.

Career development communication is crucial to retaining talent, and recruiters have this fact in mind when they try to woo your top people away. High-performing employees need to know that development opportunities exist within your company and that their managers will work with them to make the most of those opportunities. This article features concrete advice from talent-management and retention experts on how to make career development conversations less difficult and more effective—for you and for your employees.

Gary, Loren. "Do People Want to Work for You?" *Harvard Management Update*, March 2004.

A company's reputation as an employer of choice is only as strong as its individual managers. Companies know that their profitability improves when potential jobseekers consider them an employer of choice. That's why they've devoted so much energy in recent years to developing not only the recruitment practices that will enable them to find the top talent, but also the retention practices that will keep current employees' hearts and minds engaged. Organization-wide initiatives are not enough, however. A company cannot become an employer of choice unless it has managers of choice.

Harvard Business School Publishing. "Employee Retention: What Managers Can Do." *Harvard Management Update,* April 2000.

Losing too many good people? This article focuses on what managers can do to improve retention rates in their divisions, departments, or teams. Includes guidelines for recognizing the early warning signs of defection, as well as hiring right in the first place—a key first step to retention.

Hewlett, Sylvia Ann and Carolyn Buck Luce. "Off-Ramps and On-Ramps: Keeping Talented Women on the Road to Success." *Harvard Business Review* OnPoint Enhanced Edition. Boston: Harvard Business School Publishing, March 2005.

Most professional women step off the career fast track at some point. With children to raise, elderly parents to care for, and other pulls on their time, these women are confronted with one off-ramp after another. The on-ramps for professional women to get back on track are few and far between, the authors confirm. Their new survey research reveals for the first time the extent of the problem—what percentage of highly qualified women leave work and for how long, what obstacles they face coming back, and what price they pay for their time-outs. As market and economic factors align in ways guaranteed to make talent constraints and skill shortages huge issues again, employers must learn to reverse this brain drain. Strategies for building such connections include creating reduced-hour jobs, providing flexibility in the workday and in the arc of a career, removing the stigma of taking time off, refusing to burn bridges, offering outlets for altruism, and nurturing women's ambition.

Ross, Judith A. "Dealing with the Real Reasons People Leave." *Harvard Management Update*, August 2005.

Although most people tell human resources they are leaving for more money or a better opportunity, 88% change jobs because of negative factors in their current workplace, ranging from subpar people management to toxic culture. With the U.S. Department of Labor predicting potential labor shortages through the year 2012, managers must discontinue this ostrich-like behavior and address employee turnover head on. At plenty of firms, for example, retention remains a concern only when executives fear that valued employees may seriously be considering leaving. But this way of thinking dooms a company to failure, as it ignores all the opportunities to keep people from even thinking about leaving. Indeed, the retention war begins at the hiring stage—with companies recruiting employees whose talents and interests fit with both the short- and long-term needs of the organization. And once employees are in the door, the battle to keep them should commence immediately.

Ross, Judith A. "Five Ways to Boost Retention." *Harvard Management Update*, April 2008.

In boom times and slow times alike, you need to keep your best people. This article spells out five proven practices to help you keep your most talented employees: Provide paths to advancement by keeping employees informed about your company's direction. Enrich employees' experience by giving them ownership of their work and the freedom to take risks. Express appreciation. Counteract stress by creating a culture that promotes work/life balance. And foster employee trust by ensuring that executives convey clear objectives and the confidence that employees can achieve them.

Books

Cappelli, Peter. *Talent on Demand: Managing Talent in the Age of Uncertainty*. Boston: Harvard Business Press, 2008.

Managers everywhere acknowledge that finding, retaining, and growing talent counts among their toughest business challenges. Yet to address this concern, many are turning to talent management practices that no longer work because the environment they were tailored to no longer exists. This book examines the talent management and retention problem through a new lens. Drawing from numerous company examples, it gives you ideas and tools to ensure that your organization has the talent it needs—when it needs it.

Harris, Jim and Joan Brannick. *Finding and Keeping Great Employees*. New York: AMACOM, 1999.

Based on extensive research into best practices at a wide variety of organizations, this book shows how companies can leverage their core purpose and corporate cultures to attract and retain top talent. As the authors explain, clarifying purpose and culture lets companies align employees and strengthen commitment and motivation.

Michaels, Ed, Helen Handfield-Jones, and Beth Axelrod. *The War for Talent*. Boston: Harvard Business School Press, 2001.

In 1998, a landmark *McKinsey Quarterly* article exposed the "war for talent" as a critical business challenge and a fundamental driver of corporate performance. Now, just when you thought it was over, the authors present compelling evidence that the war for talent will persist over the next two decades despite the twists and turns of the economy. In this definitive guide, the authors present a strategic view of what managers must do to win the war for talent. Drawing on their five years of research, including surveys of 13,000 executives and case studies of 27 companies (including Amgen, GE, PerkinElmer, and The Home Depot), they map out five bold imperatives for attracting, developing, and retaining the very best people. Most importantly, they show that great talent management has more to do with a pervasive "talent mind-set" than it does with better HR processes.

Waldroop, James and Timothy Butler. *Maximum Success: Changing the 12 Behavior Patterns That Keep You from Getting Ahead*. New York: Currency/Doubleday, 2000.

People stay in jobs in which they're successful, and managers can encourage them by helping employees succeed. This book describes 12 all-too-common problematic behaviors that hold people back from achieving their full career potential and explains how employees can both understand and modify their behavior to get on track.

eLearning

Harvard Business School Publishing. Case in Point. Boston: Harvard Business School Publishing, 2004.

Case in Point is a flexible set of online cases, designed to help prepare middle- and senior-level managers for a variety of leadership challenges. These short, reality-based scenarios provide sophisticated content to create a focused view into the realities of the life of a leader. Your managers will experience: Aligning Strategy, Removing Implementation Barriers, Overseeing Change, Anticipating Risk, Ethical Decisions, Building a Business Case, Cultivating Customer Loyalty, Emotional Intelligence, Developing a Global Perspective, Fostering Innovation, Defining Problems, Selecting Solutions, Managing Difficult Interactions, The Coach's Role, Delegating for Growth, Managing Creativity, Influencing Others, Managing Performance, Providing Feedback, and Retaining Talent.

Sources for Retaining Employees

The following sources aided in development of this book:

Butler, Timothy and James Waldroop. "Job Sculpting: The Art of Retaining Your Best People." *Harvard Business Review.* September–October 1999.

The Center for Organizational Research. *A Research Report on the Brave New World of Recruiting and Retention: Facts, Trends, Practices, and Strategies.* Lexington, MA: Linkage Inc., 2000.

Dobbs, Kevin. "Winning the Retention Game." *Training,* September 1999.

"Employee Retention: What Managers Can Do." *Harvard Management Update,* April 2000.

Erickson, Tamara. *Plugged In: The Generation Y Guide to Thriving at Work.* Boston: Harvard Business Press, 2008.

Erickson, Tamara. "The Leaders We Need Now." *Harvard Business Review,* May 2010.

Gendron, Marie. "Keys to Retaining Your Best Managers in a Tight Job Market." *Harvard Management Update,* June 1998.

Half, Robert. *Finding, Hiring, and Keeping the Best Employees*. New York: John Wiley & Sons, 1993.

Harris, Jim and Joan Brannick. *Finding and Keeping Great Employees*. New York: AMACOM, 1999.

Herman, Roger E. *Keeping Good People: Strategies for Solving the #1 Problem Facing Business Today*. Winchester, VA: Oakhill Press, 1999.

"How to Keep Your 50-Somethings" (Managing the Labor Shortage: Part 1). *Harvard Management Update,* September 1999.

Kaye, Beverly and Sharon Jordan-Evans. *Love 'Em or Lose 'Em: Getting Good People to Stay*. San Francisco: Berrett-Koehler, 1999.

Kaye, Beverly and Sharon Jordan-Evans. "Retention: Tag, You're It!" *Training & Development,* April 2000.

Leading Across the Ages. Interactive online course. CD-ROM. Harvard Business Publishing, 2009.

Littman, Margaret. "The Best Bosses Tell All." *Working Woman,* October 2000.

Logan, Jill Klobucar. "Retention Tangibles." *Training & Development,* April 2000.

Meister, Jeanne C., and Karie Willyerd. "Mentoring Millenials." *Harvard Business Review,* May 2010.

Moore, Jo-Ellen. "Are You Burning Out Valuable Resources?" *HR Magazine,* January 1999.

New England Human Resources Association seminar. Providence, RI, November 2000.

Olesen, Margaret. "What Makes Employees Stay." *Training & Development,* October 1999.

Roth, Daniel. "My Job at the Container Store." *Fortune,* January 10, 2000.

Ruch, Will. "How to Keep Gen-X Employees from Becoming X-Employees." *Training & Development,* April 2000.

Salopek, Jennifer J. "Career Centered." *Training & Development,* April 2000.

Wagner, Stacey. "Retention: Finders, Keepers." *Training & Development,* August 2000.

Waldroop, James. Personal communication. November 8, 2000.

Waldroop, James and Timothy Butler. *Maximum Success: Changing the 12 Behavior Patterns That Keep You from Getting Ahead.* New York: Currency/Doubleday, 2000.

Waterman, Jr., Robert H., Judith A. Waterman, and Betsy A. Collard. "Toward a Career-Resilient Work Force." *Harvard Business Review,* July-August 1994.

How to Order

Harvard Business School Press publications are available world-wide from your local bookseller or online retailer.

You can also call:
1-800-668-6780

Our product consultants are available to help you 8:00 a.m.–6:00 p.m., Monday–Friday, Eastern Time. Outside the U.S. and Canada, call: 617-783-7450.

Please call about special discounts for quantities greater than ten.

You can order online at:
www.HBSPress.org